Leverage

Leverage

The Science of Turning Setbacks into Springboards

CLAIRE DOROTIK-NANA M.A.

ISBN: 1508634297
ISBN 13: 9781508634294
Library of Congress Control Number: 2015903248
CreateSpace Independent Publishing Platform
North Charleston, SC

Contents

Introduction

Today there is no shortage of adversity. In fact, recent data from the National Institute of Mental Health reports that six out of ten women and five out of ten men will face one or more major crises in their lifetime. And when they do, there will be plenty of resources—from self-help books to websites, podcasts, and "coaches"—to help them quickly move past it. Yet, the question remains, *is moving past adversity quickly really the best approach?* Self-help gurus, sports coaches, and the media tell us that we should minimize our setbacks, overcome adversity, and quickly bounce back from failure. That should we miss our mark, make a mistake, say the wrong thing, wear the wrong clothes, or show up to the wrong meeting—all things quite possible—we should not waste any time getting right back on track. These mishaps should be reframed, filed away, overcome, or—whatever self-help lingo we may want to insert here—moved past. Even catastrophic events—the kind that shatter our very fundamental beliefs and assumptions about ourselves, the world, and everything we know—should be quickly overcome. Our resilience depends on it, or so we are told.

Yet for all of this talk about bouncing back from our setbacks, are we shortchanging ourselves? Is there something we can learn from adversity, struggle, or strife? Is it possible that struggling with what ails, confuses, derails, and even shatters us offers us something? In searching for new meaning in the aftermath of trauma, can we also find a way to cope that goes much further than providing us protection—known as resilience—against further setbacks? Maybe in the struggle, and not necessarily the victory, there is something to be learned, a strength to be gained, skills to be perfected, and confidence to be reinforced. Should the victory come too quickly, perhaps we also become too focused on simply getting past the struggle and miss the opportunity that the good fight offers us. We may also place value on the very thing that causes us to lose focus. Perhaps in concentrating too intently on the victory, we are forgetting the journey.

Because the journey is not the victory and, in fact, may be nothing like victory. Instead, the journey may be rife with misses, failures, setbacks, disappointments, and defeats. It may also include tremendous joy, exultation, and reverie. The journey, like anything else, will include both highs and lows, and sometimes one will come right after the other. The hope is that for all of life's challenges and moments of glory, there will also be growth.

And this growth is dependent on the struggle, not the victory. Surprising new research in the field of posttraumatic growth has evidenced that it is not the absence of negative outcomes in the aftermath of trauma that marks the path of growth but rather that both positive and negative symptoms signify the very cognitive processes that characterize growth. It is when we can see both the good and the bad—called dialectical thinking—that we also recognize that growth is paradoxical. That we may be more vulnerable, and yet stronger, in ways we never knew possible. We may be more wary in relationships and yet develop deep connections with those closest to us. We may feel as if our path is blocked, but we may also find new, more meaningful paths.

The victory may or may not be won. But the struggle persists. It persists because there is something more meaningful than gold medals, new records, fame, or glory—and that is the pursuit of something much larger than any material gain. It is the search for meaning and purpose in the face of adversity. It is the deep human drive to challenge ourselves, perfect our skills, and to fight the good fight. It is knowing that, right or wrong, we gave it our all. It is continuing on, when the path seems blocked, to carve new paths. It is facing our vulnerabilities in the hope that we will come out stronger. It is the relationships we form along the way that will sustain us, forever unshakeable. And it is the relentless forward push, even when the odds seem insurmountable and victory seems impossible. Because, in the end, the victory is uncertain, but the journey will go on. Because, in the end, it is not the end, but the path we take, the choices we make, and the desire to face the struggle for the promise of growth.

Surprisingly, there are some people who appear to embrace the struggle, perfecting their skills against the twists and turns life deals them. Becoming adept, these people engage in the challenge because they know it will lead to mastery, and not necessarily mastery in overcoming the struggle, but mastery in facing the struggle. They don't fear failure, because the game is not being played to win or lose, it is being played to get better. Because they are not dependent on winning, they are open to any new opportunities life presents, and they are also not afraid to take on a challenge, as it is a rich source of mastery. Those in the field of positive psychology would say these people are "flourishing," while those who study trauma might say they have experienced posttraumatic growth. In either case, the data present the same story; that is, these people defy everything we know about the way adversity and trauma are supposed to affect a person.

But look more closely. Studies of posttraumatic growth show that people who experience growth after a traumatic event *outweigh* those who experience PTSD. As these studies demonstrate, more people experience trauma as a trigger that sets off a cascade of growth across several life domains than those who experience it in just the opposite way—as a trigger for a cascade of distressing symptoms. This suggests that it's not simply that some people can grow through facing challenge but rather that the way we look at challenge—as well as trauma, setbacks, and failures—is flawed. It is flawed because those who are trained in psychology and treating trauma are trained in a model that simply doesn't fit the data anymore.

I am not suggesting that there is no such thing as PTSD, as it is a very real and distressing condition. However, studies on posttraumatic growth also show something very interesting when it comes to trauma-related distress symptoms, like those in PTSD. Many trauma survivors report growth outcomes while still reporting distress symptoms. This means that growth begins before distress ends. In fact, the paradoxical nature of growth is consistently demonstrated in the research on post-traumatic growth. That is to say that a person can feel stronger and yet more vulnerable, or as if life is more fragile but also appreciated much more. And yet what is focused on in the therapist's office, as well as in society, is the victory. Overcoming the setback, minimizing the failure, and quickly bouncing back all insinuate the same message: overcoming is more important than learning. Because the learning comes in the challenge, the enhancement of skill, the atonement of mastery, and the engagement itself—that is, the willingness to take on the challenge even when success seems out of reach.

What this book argues is not just that the way we treat adversity and setbacks is outdated and out of focus. When we seek to only treat distress symptoms, we suppress the deep human drive to master challenge and grow as a result. And when we focus on overcoming setbacks, bouncing back, and winning the game, we also suppress the intrinsic human need to engage. Presented are two central tenets. First, that adversity and struggle are growth-enhancing opportunities and that the way we treat adversity today is flawed. Second, the process of struggling with the adversity—and not necessarily overcoming it, as evidenced by the data on the paradoxical nature of growth—is more growth enhancing than the victory itself.

Section One

One

What Are Setbacks, and Why Do They Matter?

"Our greatest glory is not in never failing,
but in rising up every time we fail."
— Ralph Waldo Emerson

Pulling on his racing shirt—the one that had successfully carried him across the finish line of his last attempt—he began the routine. Almost automatic now, he'd specifically tried not to change anything for fear that he'd invite "bad mojo" or throw off his vibe in some way. The toe socks—the ones with five small "fingers" for the toes—had been bought (double thick, of course). He'd already learned that the thin ones can cause blisters, which can end a race like this. The shoes were broken in—the recommended twenty-five miles—and he chose not to wear the gaiters. He hadn't trained with them, and he didn't think the small stretch of Dri-FIT fabric pulled over his ankles to keep the rocks out of his shoes would matter too much today. He'd been told the course had roots—lots of roots—but not rocks, so he should be OK.

The shorts, undershorts, shirt, and visor were all well-worn, having been trained in all year. These, he'd been told, should be well broken in. And there they lay, with the sunglasses on top, and the long-sleeve

Dri-FIT—which he intended to remove before starting—draped on the bed, ready. Beside them lay a large plastic bag with the Gu. Fifteen packets to be exact. And all in one flavor: vanilla. He'd tried them all, as he'd been told that the jelly-like substance was what all the athletes used and that it provided the best quick fuel to the muscles. But they all came back up after twenty miles—except for the vanilla. He didn't understand why, but he wasn't about to change. Next to the plastic bag of Gu lay another bag with fifteen packets of powdered sports recovery drink and a small plastic bottle. The plan was to drink one bottle for every packet of Gu. After twenty miles, he'd start taking in "real food." Although he didn't know quite what would be available—these events usually offered anything from pizza to candy—he'd also brought his own. Three bags of pita bread, two tubs of hummus, one jar of peanut butter, and two large bags of pretzels—he wanted to make sure he had enough for himself and his crew.

And he'd told them just what he needed. No pampering. He had a job to do, and he came here to do it. Just prepare the supplies, don't ask him how he's doing, and don't let him stay too long. He has to keep moving. The crew—like all the supplies—had been well prepared.

So it began. Slowly at first, but loop after loop of the 3.1 mile course he started accumulating miles. Three, six, nine, twelve. He'd reminded himself not to count. At twenty-nine, there were just too many. So he flipped on his iPod, settled into a rhythm—a mix between power walking and jogging—and before he knew it, he was over fifty miles in. More than halfway done in what seemed like the blink of an eye. And it had been without event. He'd tripped a few times on the roots, but he'd expected that. He'd gotten a little warm in the heat of the day, but he'd also trained for that. And the knee that had given him trouble in the past had been surprisingly quiet.

But then, without warning, it hit him. At first he didn't know what it was, but *something* was different. It started with *why? Why am I doing this?* It was a question he'd asked himself many times. And he thought he knew the answer, but today it was gone. Instead, there was another question: *Does this really matter?* Yet as he searched for a way to explain this to himself, he started to doubt. *Maybe I can't go another fifty miles. Maybe I don't even want to.* And he tried to shake it off. *Of course I want this. I trained all year for this.* But questions and the doubt wouldn't go away. And then his step slowed, and for the first time, he felt tired—really tired. He tried to regroup, telling his crew to give him "time to think," and he sat down, stared at his feet, and looked for answers. His crew knew not to ask. But others didn't. *What's wrong? Are you OK? Are you injured?* He told them he was fine, and that was true—in the physical sense.

But the doubt had crept in like an unwelcome guest. And then it had taken over. And as much as he had tried, he couldn't shake it off. It wasn't just that he thought he couldn't go on; it was that it was hard—really hard—and maybe he didn't want to. And so he quit. Just that like that, a year's worth of training, countless supplies, time spent preparing, hoping, dreaming, all down the drain in a matter of minutes.

For many of us, the story sounds too familiar. We start with an inspired goal, and we're full of ambition, passion, and drive. We check our schedules, organize our lives, and plan our approach. We dedicate enormous amounts of time and energy, all toward a singular mission. But then somewhere along the way, something happens. Maybe someone close to us expresses doubt. Maybe we receive a rejection, hit a stumbling block, or encounter a problem. Maybe we even experience our own doubt. And just like that, progress halts.

While a setback can be defined as a halt in progress, the meaning of a setback, for many of us, is much larger.

Setbacks Make Us Question Our Fundamental Beliefs

When what we are doing stops moving us toward our goal, when our approach is questioned or criticized, when our reality suddenly changes such that we cannot go on as we were, we question the very beliefs with which we advanced upon our goal. This is what setbacks do; they make us question our fundamental assumptions about the way things *should* work. Maybe we encounter truths that don't fit into our understanding of what is supposed to happen.

A successful CEO and former teacher, Rob once shared with me that as soon as his principal learned he was gay, he was fired. In one short meeting with the woman, everything he believed about teaching—that he had gone into it for noble purposes; that it was about helping children learn; that his passion, drive, and commitment would be valued—was shattered. Being gay was not supposed to matter. But it did. And this information caused Rob to question everything he had thought about the profession and even about himself. *Was he wrong for wanting to be a teacher? Had he been naïve? Was he wrong, or bad, for being gay? Was he harmful to students, as his principal had suggested?* These, and many more, were the questions that he asked himself countless times.

Sometimes it is our expectations that are challenged as well. If what we expect to happen does not, or how we expect to feel does not materialize, we question our expectations. We may question not just what we expect from others but from ourselves as well. If what we thought would make us happy doesn't, we may wonder if our calculations about ourselves were wrong.

A chef and former family practitioner, Kevin shared with me that he thought being a doctor was the way to happiness, that once he achieved that, he would be happy and have everything he wanted in life. Yet once he was there, Kevin was miserable and found he hated medicine, the long hours, the constant worry over his patients, the liability risk, and the enormous financial cost of his education. And he, too, questioned whether he had made the right decision. But on a much deeper level, Kevin questioned how much he really knew about himself. He wondered how he could miscalculate so completely what would bring happiness to his life.

Kevin questioned what happiness really was. And he questioned his ability to make any other decisions for fear that he would miscalculate those as well.

We may even lose trust in others, in ourselves, and in the world when our paths seem blocked. If we have been betrayed by others, we may wonder if we were wrong for trusting them. We may wonder if we missed something and how able we are to decipher if anyone really is trustworthy. We may wonder if we ever really learned to trust in the first place or if the relationships we had were truly honest. We may even question what relationships are supposed to be.

One woman, Sally, shared her mistrust with me after her husband of seventeen years committed suicide. She wondered if he had ever been honest with her. She wondered if she ever really knew him. She wondered if she hadn't asked the right questions or hadn't been observant enough. Sally questioned what the meaning of marriage and "'til death do us part" is supposed to include. But most deeply, Sally questioned her trust. *Could she trust anyone now? If her husband—her most trusted partner—hadn't been honest with her, how could she trust anyone?* These were questions she simply couldn't avoid, as they defined everything she knew about trust.

And yet there is something else that happens with setbacks. We ruminate about them.[1] Conceivably, if every setback could have been predicted, we might not. But setbacks, by nature, take us by surprise. And because they cause us to question fundamental concepts and beliefs—like trust, honor, and honesty—we think about them, rehash and replay them in an effort to find understanding.[2] It's the cognitive disruption that we are trying to piece together, and the ultimate question we all ask is, Why did this happen? It's the way in which things we don't understand impact us, but it is also the inherent desire that we all have for some level of homeostatic balance. Because homeostatic balance allows us to predict events, make adjustments, and avoid being taken by surprise. This is the brain's way of offering some protection against further cognitive disruption. Presumably, if setbacks could be prevented, there would be no cognitive disruption and no beliefs to be reconsidered.

Setbacks have a Profound Impact

But there might be another reason why we rehash setbacks. Bad events have a different impact on the brain than good events. Roy F. Baumeister, a professor of social psychology at Florida State University, states, "Bad emotions, bad parents, and bad feedback have more impact than good ones. Bad impressions and bad stereotypes are quicker to form and more resistant to disconfirmation than good ones."[3] Professor Baumeister explains that losing money, being abandoned by friends, and receiving criticism will have a greater impact than winning money, making friends, or receiving praise.[4]

Baumeister's work is seconded by Amabile (2011), who reported that the negative effect on happiness of a setback at work was more than twice as strong as the positive effect of an event that signaled progress. And the power of a setback to increase frustration is over three times as strong as the power of progress to decrease frustration.[5]

The effect that bad events have on our brains might be explained partly by the way in which our memories work. Memories that are linked to highly charged emotions, such as fear, worry, and rejection, are encoded differently in the brain from memories that are linked to positive emotions such as pleasure, happiness, and gratitude.[6]

The activity of emotionally enhanced memory retention is part of human evolution and would have proved to be an adaptive response to threatening events, as survival depended on the reinforcement of behavioral patterns provoked by life-and-death situations. This evolutionary process is also what we now know as the fight-or-flight response.

Artificially inducing this response through traumatic physically or emotionally threatening events essentially creates the same physiological condition that heightens memory retention by exciting neurochemical

activity affecting areas of the brain responsible fo'
ing memory.[7] Using a variety of stimuli, this mem'
emotion has been duplicated in a large number o.

Items that have high emotional relevance are also typ..
higher attendance with greater cognitive engagement, especian,
when attention is limited, which suggests that we process emotional
information with greater priority.[9, 10] Typically, when emotional information involves threatening stimuli, the adaptive—and automatic—
response is to process it quickly.[11] A second postulation, however, is
that highly distressing emotions demand more cognitive focus as they
generate more distress.[12] Much in the same way that a screaming child
demands attention, our distressing emotions demand our brain's
attention.

Emotionally charged memories also appear to have a stronger
imprint on our brains over time, and the likelihood with which memories will be consolidated, creating a permanent record. A number of
studies show that, over time, memories for neutral stimuli decrease but
memories for arousing stimuli remain the same or improve.[13]

It could also be possible that in processing the negative memories
more, we invest more effort in elaboration of those memories. Elaboration
refers to the process of establishing links between newly encountered
information and previously stored information. This process, which seeks
to find meaning and make associations between events, enhances memory.[14] It is when we allocate more cognitive attention to the central details
of a distressing event that memory is likely to be enhanced.[15]

The case for paying attention to setbacks, and the effect they have
on us, can be made not just because negative events appear to have a
greater impact on memory and retention and demand more cognitive attention than do positive ones, but because the process is highly
automatic. Once the physiological system is charged and threat is perceived, we don't have a choice about what we pay attention to. This is
also the reason flashbacks and nightmares are automatic, unconscious
responses to troubling events, and it isn't until the threat is resolved,

the emotional response contained, that attention can be devoted to something else.

Setbacks are the Forground of Adaptation

Due to the troubling effect that hypervigilance and unconscious replaying of disturbing events have on us, we tend to focus on quickly resolving setbacks. Certainly, when distress symptoms cause a disturbance in functioning, this should be the case. But setbacks matter because they incite a critical reconsideration of fundamental beliefs, values, and goals. When what we used to assume about the world, ourselves, and others can no longer be integrated into our existing understanding, we must adapt. An example of this is a high-school football star who is highly recruited and has very strong college scholarship potential but who is suddenly sidelined by a career-ending injury. Here is someone who has invested everything into one singular goal: to play football professionally. And yet without warning that option is removed. Injury simply didn't figure into the plan and doesn't work with playing professionally. The only choice is to reconsider the options. And along with options, beliefs, values, and goals will also be reconsidered. This is the process of adaptation—and it is a crucial process.

It is through adaptation that we make critical decisions about what is most important to us, often making dramatic changes in the way we live our lives. When we must accept that our lives have been dramatically interrupted, we often ponder fundamental questions about our values, asking ourselves why this—the setback—happened. We question our actions. We question our beliefs. We question our values. *Had these things led us down the wrong path? Had we been blind to the looming setback?* And these are fundamental questions without which reconsideration does not happen.

And reconsideration—like setbacks—matters, because it is how adaptation happens. Reconsideration allows us to look clearly at our approach; to closely examine our assumptions, thoughts, and beliefs;

to ask critical questions; and to accept the way in which these things do not work under the present circumstances. It is through this process that knowledge about what must be changed is revealed. And this is how we make critical adaptations.

But this process is also evolutionary. As Tim Harford explains in his brilliant book *Adapt: Why Success Always Starts with Failure,* "the evolutionary algorithm—of variation and selection, repeated—searches for solutions in a world where problems keep changing, trying all sorts of variants and doing more of what works."[16] Harford goes on to describe what he calls a "fitness landscape"—a flat landscape divided into a grid of several billion squares, each containing a document of information: a recipe for a particular strategy. The information can be biological in nature—such as the genetic material for a bird, cow, or human—but it can also represent things like recipes for dinner: some produce salad, some produce poison, and some produce nauseating dishes. But some, Harford explains, "might also contain business strategies like different ways to run an airline, or a fast food chain."

Harford further describes success and failure in a fitness landscape represented by altitude—where peaks represent success and valleys represent failures. McDonald's might be a very large peak, and the newspaper industry might be sinking into a valley. In other areas, take running shoes for example, some peaks come and go—like the overbuilt extra-padded shoes that temporarily went out of favor when the minimalist shoe market exploded, and everybody wanted to run as close to barefoot as possible, only to return when running barefoot was linked to a high incidence of injuries. Yet the landscape is constantly shifting, and some peaks move faster than others. And the reason evolution works, as Harford explains, is because as opposed to exhaustive, time-consuming searches for the highest peaks, it produces solutions that are adaptive and "work for now." If the landscape changes, as it often does, these solutions will die off—like the weeding out of extinction—and the process will begin again, driven by variation and selection.

Much like evolution, making critical adaptations is an ongoing process and one that depends on setbacks. With each setback, new information is gleaned, strategies that do not work are weeded out, and ones that do work come to the fore. The result is a refined and improved approach—and one that reflects a changing landscape.

TWO

THE SHATTERED VASE IS THE FERTILE GROUND

*"Never be afraid to fall apart because it is an opportunity to
rebuild yourself the way you wish you had been all along."*

— RAE SMITH

Psychiatrist John Bowlby describes childhood as a time when children develop working models that allow them to navigate relationships, draw conclusions about the way things work, predict the future, and construct plans. Over time, Bowlby continues, a child begins to separate the way he sees himself from the way he sees others and incorporates an understanding for things that are outside of himself. Recent decades in developmental psychological research have suggested that the formation of the mental world is enabled by the infant–parent interpersonal interaction, which allows a child to develop a "theory of mind."[1]

Noted psychoanalyst and former president of the International Psychoanalytical Association, Joseph Sandler calls this the "representational world," the constellation of organized, enduring impressions culled from experience that serve as a cognitive map comprised of symbols for understanding everything from what a toaster feels like or how peanut butter tastes to what Aunt Martha's breath smells like.[2] Images created allow a child to develop a way to navigate the world before he is able to verbally describe it. Adaptively, a child who understands the effect things have on him—why not to touch the toaster when the red light is on—is also able to respond in ways that create desired responses, exhibiting a sense of control over the environment.

But children also develop representations of people—particularly care-givers—and from very early on, they begin organizing a set of assumptions about them. This set of assumptions, which the British psychologist C. M. Parkes calls the "assumptive world," is "a strongly held set of assumptions about the world and the self which is confidently maintained and used as a means of recognizing, planning, and acting."[3] Parkes goes on to describe the adaptive relationship between assumptions and experience. Over time, Parkes notes, assumptions that can be confirmed through experience will remain, and assumptions that do not hold true against experience will be let go. What fits into the assumptive world are only those assumptions that "are learned and confirmed by the experience of many years."

While others have called the assumptive world "a network of diverse theories and representations" that "reflect and guide our interactions in the world," psychologist Ronnie Janoff-Bulman proposes that of the multitude of representations and assumptions that can be developed through experience, there are three basic ones: the world is benevolent, life events have meaning, and the self is worthy.[4]

The Assumptive World is Often Wrong

Bulman purports that people go to great lengths to maintain these beliefs—even to their detriment. She cites the story of Job—repeated and unwarranted hardship—and the attention this story receives as evidence that these beliefs exist. Bulman suggests that we pay attention to stories such as these precisely *because* they violate our core beliefs that life is inherently good and that bad things should not happen.[5]

Evidence for this tendency exists not just in historical accounts but in modern-day media as well—that events such as mass shootings, murders, and natural disasters captivate us. And they do because they defy what we know about the way things are *supposed* to happen. Inherently, we are oriented to believe that the world is safe, people are not dangerous, and there is a predictability in life that can be depended upon.

For a child, navigating the world depends on this belief. As the renowned child psychiatrist Ronald Fairburn—often referred to as the father of object relations theory—explains, it's better to be a bad child in a good world than a good child in a bad world. Constructing much of what he knew from Freud's theory of mind, Fairburn identified how, through experience, children internalize events—particularly abuse—and develop "moral defenses" in order to continue interacting in the world. One such moral defense, Fairburn explained, is the tendency seen in survivors of abuse to take all the bad upon themselves, each believing he is morally bad so his caretaker can be regarded as good.[6] The reason a child would do this, Fairburn asserts, is the same reason Bulman believes people pay attention to Job's story—to maintain the belief that the world is good.

As adults, we call this cognitive bias. Thanks to Daniel Kahneman and Amos Tversky, who first introduced the term in 1972, we now understand cognitive biases as mental shortcuts designed to account for the mind's limited information-processing capacity, to reduce mental noise, and to infer social and emotional motivations.[7] While it may be an overgeneralization and a bias to believe that all men wearing hooded sweatshirts are dangerous, it may also save enormous amounts of time in deciphering *which* hooded-sweatshirt-wearing men are dangerous. Particularly in the case of life-and-death events, biases can be adaptive.[8, 9]

Kahneman and Tversky initially recognized these biases while studying peoples' inability to reason intuitively on tests that examined the likelihood of events. Tversky, Kahneman, and colleagues repeatedly demonstrated several ways in which human judgments and decisions differ from answers that would seem most rational. For example, participants were asked to "judge the frequency or likelihood" of an occurrence by the extent to which the event "resembles the typical case." In the "Linda Problem," participants were given a description of Linda that suggests she might well be a feminist (e.g., she is said to be concerned about discrimination and social-justice issues). They were then asked whether they thought Linda was more likely to be an "(a) bank teller" or a "(b) bank teller and active in the feminist movement." A majority chose answer *b*. This error (mathematically, answer *b* cannot be more likely than answer *a*) is an example of what Tversky and Kahneman call the conjunction fallacy. This tendency, one of the identified cognitive biases, describes the way in which people will choose a response because it seems more "representative" or typical of persons who might fit a description, while ignoring relevant statistical probability.[10, 11]

Tversky and Kahneman explained cognitive biases in terms of heuristics—or simple, efficient rules that people often use to form judgments and make decisions. Heuristics involve mental shortcuts that provide swift estimates about the possibility of uncertain occurrences. And while they are simple for the brain to compute, heuristics sometimes introduce "severe and systematic errors." The representativeness heuristic, for example, may lead to errors such as activating stereotypes and inaccurate judgments of others.[12] Perhaps in classifying *all* men wearing hooded sweatshirts as dangerous—or *all* people of any race, culture, or gender—as ascribing to a particular characteristic, we are missing the ones who are not.

Biases Maintain Subjective Reality

Drawn in an illogical fashion, these biases, Tversky and Kahneman note, seek to maintain a "subjective reality" that aligns with our perception of the world.[13] If we have been hurt by men in hooded sweatshirts, our reality is that men such as this are dangerous, and inferences we make will serve to confirm this belief.[14] Constructing our social reality in this way—all the while ignoring the objective input—then dictates how we behave. For this reason, cognitive biases can lead to perceptual distortion, inaccurate judgment, illogical interpretation, and what Daniel Gilbert, author of *Stumbling on Happiness*, calls "cooking the facts."

As Gilbert explains, we simply interpret the facts in a way that conforms to the reality we are seeking to create. If we need to believe that we got a good deal on the new car we just bought, we will "filter out" any information pointing to the car's poor reliability and pay attention to the positive customer reviews the car receives.[15]

Cognitive biases are important to study because they lead to "systematic errors." As Tversky and Kahneman point out, they highlight the "psychological processes that underlie perception and judgment."[16] According to Kahneman and Tversky, these errors are widespread, ranging from the "sunk-cost" fallacy, which describes a retrospective cost that cannot be recovered and weighs heavily on decision making, causing people to delay changing course as a result of "money that has already been spent," to the illusory correlation, which describes the tendency to perceive a relationship between two variables that does not actually exist, such as forming a false relationship between a culture or class and negative or positive behavior. While illusory correlations affect a person's judgment of how likely something is to occur, other cognitive biases affect memory, such as consistency bias, which relates to the tendency to remember past attitudes and behavior as more similar to one's present attitudes.[17, 18]

Still other biases influence our actions—particularly the ones we take to maintain a positive self-image. Egocentric biases, and avoiding unpleasant information, both lead to cognitive dissonance, that is, a disconnect between how we see ourselves and how others see us. While we may think we are kind and generous, others may point to the times we cut in line, interrupt others, and forget to call our mothers.[19, 20, 21]

Cognitive Biases Lead to Errors in Judgment

All cognitive biases lead to errors in judgment that cause us to make decisions based on what *we think* should be true as opposed to what is *actually* true. If we think we should be able to trust the used-car salesman, we will pay attention to information that confirms that we got a good deal, all the while ignoring any evidence to the contrary. And according to Tversky and Kahneman, the more we believe that something should be true—called the belief bias—the more an argument will be biased.[22, 23]

At some level, all biases ignore reality. As Gilbert explains, even in predicting what events will lead to happiness, we make three key errors. According to Gilbert, the first involves the imagination, as the imagination tends to add and remove details, but people do not realize that key details may be fabricated or missing from the imagined scenario. We also tend to become stuck in what Gilbert called "presentism," which means imagining futures (and pasts) are more like the present than they actually will be (or were). The last error Gilbert attributes to failure to account for the "psychological immune system," which will make bad things feel not as bad as they are imagined to feel.

Yet errors in judgment attributable to cognitive biases are not isolated to individuals. Harford points to several examples to show that errors in judgment are a result of systemic cognitive biases. Harford cites the work of economist Paul Ormerod, who compared fossil records that revealed extinction patterns to the "extinction patterns" of corporations. As Harford relates,

❖ ❖ ❖

"Ormerod discovered something disturbing: it was possible to build a model that mimicked the real extinction signature of firms, and it was possible to build a model that represented firms as modestly successful planners; but it was not possible to build a model that did both. The patterns of corporate life and death are totally different from reality in the "planning is possible" model, but uncannily close to reality in the "planning is impossible" model. If companies really could plan successfully—as most of us naturally assume that they can—then the extinction signature of companies would look totally different to that of the species."[24]

The point Harford makes is that, like individuals, corporations fail when it comes to predicting what approaches will lead to success. Where individuals consistently miscalculate which choices will lead to happiness, corporations consistently miscalculate which approaches will lead to profit.

While Harford cautions that Ormerod's model is mathematical in nature, and while we should not jump to conclusions about the data, we should consider the crucial finding that in a competitive environment, many corporate decisions do not prevent the losses they are designed to prevent. This is the reason, Harford explains, that when a psychologist named Phillip Tetlock interviewed nearly three hundred experts, asking some 27,450 questions of prediction—everything from which political figures would succeed or fail, which businesses could be expected to thrive, and what market trends would emerge—the data revealed that the "experts'" predictions were no better than those of a control group. Of expert judgment and by the history of "excellent" companies that so often lose their way, Tetlock concluded, we are blinder than we think.

What the work of Tversky, Kahneman, and Gilbert reveal on an individual level, Harford's work reveals on a much larger scale. That is, we are primed to cling to our beliefs—*even when they prove to be wrong*. We simply don't like changing our minds. This is why we will elect George W. Bush, who promised to "stay the course," and send John Kerry, who earned the label of a "flip-flopper," back to the drawing board.

The reason we cling to our beliefs, Harford explains, is an immunity to feedback that, like Gilbert's "psychological immune system," keeps us from making the necessary adaptations to reflect the changing circumstances around us. On an evolutionary level, adaptations promote survival; on an individual level, they make happiness more likely; and on an economic level, they are the foundation of prosperity. Had adaptation occurred, Harford argues, the Soviet economy might not have failed. Yet what the Soviet system had on a national scale, many of us have on an individual level, and that is what Harford calls a "pathological inability to adapt." They failed because they could not tolerate changing the approach—even when it clearly wasn't working.

But how could they have known? Feedback in the Soviet Union was ruthlessly suppressed. The reason could possibly be explained as intrinsic to a communist system, but it could also be endemic to human nature. As Harford explains, "There is a limit to how much honest feedback most leaders really want to hear; and because we know this, most of us sugarcoat our opinions whenever we speak to a powerful person." But we probably don't only sugarcoat our feedback when we speak to leaders.

The work of Tversky and Kahneman shows that we also employ denial when interpreting information to ourselves. Following the plays of several thousand chess players, Tversky and Kahneman showed that players consistently fail to acknowledge losses, and they point to players' tendency to take wild risks after loss as evidence. In their words, "a person who has not made peace with his losses is likely to accept gambles that would be unacceptable to him otherwise."[25]

Setbacks Reveal Our Biases

And this is the case we can make for setbacks—and not the small ones. Setbacks force a fundamental collision of two realities: that which we would like to maintain (our subjective reality) and that which is actually occurring (the objective reality). According to psychologist Stephen

Joseph, author of *What Doesn't Kill Us: The New Psychology of Posttraumatic Growth*, a setback, or traumatic experience, causes a person's life story to rupture and shatters assumptions about ourselves, others, and the world. Setbacks, by their very nature, violate our beliefs about the way things are *supposed* to happen. What results are two separate experiences that are in contradiction. On the one hand, we want to believe that the world is safe, people are trustworthy, and we are worthy, yet being rejected, losing a loved one, and being in an unexpected accident all contradict these beliefs.[26]

Especially when setbacks are of the magnitude that we cannot ignore—being uncontrollable, life threatening, and irreversible—they force an upheaval of our very fundamental beliefs about the world, who we are, and how we make sense of our daily lives. *This painful upheaval, and the shattering of what was, leads to the reconsideration of existing beliefs and plants the seeds for a new perspective on what really matters.*

Sara had been involved in a mass shooting in which she lost her best friend and her husband's best friend. While the theatre occupants directly in front and behind her had been killed, in a fortuitous twist of fate, she and her husband had been spared. Sara had never imagined being shot at, let alone losing those close to her in such a violent way. The events simply violated *everything* she knew of the world. She questioned the shooter's motives and wondered what would lead a person to massacre almost an entire theatre full of people. And on a very fundamental level, Sara questioned her deeply held belief that the world is safe. Yet struggling with hypervigilance and almost nightly flashbacks, she also realized that she'd taken many things for granted. She hadn't appreciated what she had until it was almost lost. Focusing on her career, making money, and proving herself, she'd "made many selfish decisions" and now realized that the way she had been living her life had not led to happiness. Sara thought the money and esteem meant happiness, but in hindsight, she realized she had been stressed "almost all the time." As Sara looked back, she now knew she'd made a fundamental miscalculation about her happiness. And after the shooting, her priorities changed. She traded her position at a large department store to open her own store, never worked past five o'clock, and began volunteering at a crisis center. In her words, "money can't replace people, and I can see that now."

And this might just be what is necessary. According to Lawrence Calhoun and Richard Tedeschi, authors of *The Handbook of Posttraumatic Growth: Research and Practice,* when we face assumptions about life that are in contradiction to our experience and cannot be integrated into our understanding, we are forced to let them go.[27] As our assumptive world unravels, we also reconsider our goals, hopes, wishes, and dreams and come to terms with our miscalculations: *that perhaps the path we were on was not actually leading to happiness.* And then we make critical adaptations. Sometimes these adaptations are the physical kind, like the sponsored athlete who becomes injured and simply "doesn't make the cut" must now find a new path, and sometimes they involve relationships, where after a loss we find ourselves valuing those close to us on a much deeper level. But all adaptations involve a critical reconsideration of our values and beliefs and a reconciliation of just where we have gone wrong—where we have miscalculated our lives.

Although painful, the shattering of existing beliefs and assumptions, complete with the "letting go" of long-held beliefs, goals, and matters of importance, is a crucial component of growth of any kind, but it is also instrumental to understanding what really matters. Perhaps this is due to what Gilbert describes as our uncanny ability to "manufacture happiness," or perhaps without first disabling beliefs and approaches that do not work—whether it is because they are outdated in the economic market, miscalculate political interests, or cannot be integrated into our belief system—the critical process of adaptation cannot occur. *And the result is not just adaptation; it's a profound connection to what really matters, and it's a profound improvement in happiness.*

Making his point, Gilbert points to several examples of people who have gone through what most of us would consider horrific events— being wrongly imprisoned for years, experiencing financial devastation, and losing a limb—yet describe themselves as happier after. While perhaps these people have "found a way" to make the best of dramatically changed circumstances, as Gilbert suggests, they may have also made the critical adaptations of growth—realizing just where they made errors in predicting happiness and making adjustments to reflect the changing landscape of their lives. Yet the result was profound and clear: they describe themselves as happier.

In evolution, we might call it culling (cutting out the traits that do not work and refining the species to promote survival), and on an individual level, we might call it upheaval (the unwinding of a belief system that no longer fits reality in service of new meanings and beliefs that reflect the changed landscape). And while it may lead to tremendous uncertainty as the assumptive world upon which we have come to depend is shattered, the critical choices we make (Harford would call this variation and selection) are the foreground of adaptation.

Three

WHEN ALL ROADS ARE BLOCKED,
WE MUST CARVE OUR OWN PATH

*"I believe that truth has only one face:
that of a violent contradiction."*

— GEORGES BATAILLE

While Socrates might have aimed to "advance the soul" of his subjects, and Kant's critical philosophy aspired to criticize knowledge rather than justify it as a measure of expanding consciousness, the conclusion is the same. Nothing is ever black and white.

At no time does this ever become more clear than when setbacks force us to reconsider and rebuild beliefs. Particularly when reality shatters everything that we know about ourselves, others, the world, and the way things are *supposed* to work, what we thought was so black and white—our beliefs—suddenly become nothing but a hazy mass of gray.

We are faced with contradictions—lots of them. Contradictions about ourselves: sure, we are strong, but at times we feel incredibly vulnerable. Contradictions about others: there are some we can trust and some we wouldn't dare. Contradictions about life itself: it is delightful, wonderful, precious, and, at the same time, heartbreakingly fragile.

And there is no choice but to accept the contradictions. When setbacks happen, especially the large ones, there is no denying them. It goes something like this: *Woman meets man of her dreams, marries, believes that marriage means love and trust forever, and then she finds him cheating. Or, man grows up in a family of firm, solid beliefs, good morals, and strong connections and believes that the world and the people in it are kind, and then in a shocking turn of events, his wife is murdered.* Some are traumatic, some are not, but setbacks allow no alternatives. What they do is provide undeniable evidence that our beliefs, and life itself, are full of contradictions.

But from these contradictions, we can also begin to develop what is called dialectical thinking—or what many would simply call wisdom.

Pointing to philosophers such as Socrates, Kant, Heraclitus, and Fichte, dialectical thinking has a place in philosophy; the point is to understand things from *multiple perspectives*—to explore the *possibilities* of knowledge before advancing to knowledge itself.

The initial and perhaps even sole task of philosophers, according to this view, is not to establish and demonstrate theories about reality but rather to subject all theories, including those about philosophy itself, to critical review and to measure their validity by how well they withstand criticism.[1, 2]

As the theory goes, we must understand how human reason works *before* applying it to sense experience.[3] We must first reconsider how our beliefs measure up against our experience and ask critical questions: *Are all people good? Is the world good? Does marriage last forever?* Only when these questions are considered can we construct new beliefs that better stand the test of our experience. While this flies in the face of science, which is concerned with only accepting beliefs that can be justified through *empirical* evidence, the rationalist view purports that reason or reflection alone is considered to be evidence for the truth or falsity of some beliefs. This reason and reflection will allow us to hold beliefs against the measuring stick of *our* experience, to test what works, let go of what does not, and ultimately arrive at beliefs that account for the contradictions we face—that the world is both good and bad, that marriage can be great and excruciating, that in love there is loss, and that we are both strong and vulnerable.

Because the truth is, in sense experience, things *are* experienced in multiple ways—especially when dealing with life's contradictions. There *is* loss in love, there *is* pain in a just world, and so on.

While we may struggle to reconcile these contradictions, the questions we ask: *What do we believe now? Does marriage mean love and trust forever? Are people really good, kind, and moral? What is the meaning of this?* are not far from the questions that Johann Gottlieb Fichte, the philosopher most closely credited with dialectical thinking, asked himself. While trying to find a bridge between Kant's critical philosophy and the idealistic view of Georg Wilhelm Freidrich Hegel, it was Fichte who concluded that the *only* choice was to dive into the experience of self-consciousness.[4] Fichte essentially pointed to the distinction between the *a priori* and *a posteriori*—that is, the phenomenon of experiencing something and the thing itself. Ultimately, he resolved the distinction by declaring that subjective reality, what we know as consciousness, has no grounding in the real world and, in fact, is not grounded in anything outside itself. That is, the way we experience things—with the conscious mind—*is its own reality.*[5]

What Fichte was saying was that it is the subjective reality that ultimately grounds us. That is, there is no resolution for contradiction outside of ourselves, and there is no objective black and white. How we resolve the contradictions that setbacks confront us with—and subsequently, how we make sense of the world—is an individual process driven internally, not externally.[6] Resolution, Fichte would have said, comes from within.

This departure from the suprasensible categories *beyond* human reason and, subsequently, embracing of consciousness as its own reality might have given way to the four tenets of what we know as Fitchean Dialectics:

1. Everything is transient and finite, existing in the medium of time.
2. Everything is composed of contradictions (opposing forces).
3. Gradual changes lead to crises, turning points when one force overcomes its opponent force (quantitative change leads to qualitative change).
4. Change is helical (spiral), not circular (negation of the negation).[7]

While today dialectical thinking is a bit of a cognitive outlier, the concept of dialectics underscores the importance of accepting that everything is in a state of constant change, and as the philosopher Heraclitus said, "No man steps in the same river twice." Heraclitus went further, however, extending his belief to the unity of opposites, stating that "the path up and down are one and the same," all existing entities being characterized by pairs of contrary properties.[8]

These contrary properties, or contradictions, define a situation in which the existence or identity of a thing (or situation) depends on the coexistence of at least two conditions that are opposite to each other.[9] These opposites are dependent on each other—black cannot exist without white, nor hot without cold—and create a tension between them, which, when completely balanced, leads to stasis. While these opposites can exist in thought or reality, there is unity within their duality, and their unity is that either one exists because the opposite is necessary for the existence of the other. This is the oneness—dependence even—that is principal to the very existence of any opposite.

This is also how many Hindu, Buddhist, Tantric, Zen, and mystic beliefs describe transcendence—that is, when something is understood as the oneness of contradictory opposites—*when the world is seen to be both good and bad, people seen as both strong and vulnerable, and life events seen as both cruel and meaningful.* But dialectics goes on to say that if we take an opposite to its very ultimate extreme and make it absolute, it actually turns into its opposite.[10] Thus if we make darkness absolute, we are blind—we can't see anything. And if we make light absolute, we are equally blind and unable to see. In psychology, the equivalent of this is to idealize something. So if we take love to its extreme and idealize it, we get morbid dependence, where our whole existence depends completely on the other person. And if we take hate to its extreme and idealize it, we get morbid counterdependence, where our whole existence again depends completely on the other person.

Dialectical Thinking Helps Us Appreciate Paradoxes

The appreciation of paradox is one of the strengths of the dialectical approach, but it is also what we do when we face the collision of our beliefs and our experiences. What we come to understand is that seeing something only one way—*the world where bad events aren't supposed to happen, a relationship that is supposed to only include love and never mistrust*—causes us to be blind. Just like staring into a light causes blindness, becoming awestruck with someone's good qualities causes us to be equally blind.

The purpose of dialectical thinking is the same—to come to a synthesis, or a combination of the opposing assertions, in service of a qualitative improvement of consciousness.[11] That is, to understand that everything is composed of contradictions. We cannot love everything about someone—that is to idealize him or her. Instead, every person has both positive and negative qualities. Similarly, we cannot hate everything about a person.

And it is here that dialectical thinking begins. That is, as according to the University of Chicago, "dialectic" can be defined as a "mode of thought, or a philosophic medium, through which contradiction becomes a starting point (rather than a dead end) for contemplation."[12]

Starting with a contradiction, and the resultant balance of the opposites, might not be the worst thing, especially when it comes to figuring out what works when starting at ground zero. Accepting contradictions allows for variation—understanding that no approach is all good or all bad and that in every attempt there is something to be gained and something to be learned. As Harford, whom I referenced in chapter 1, points out, some of the greatest innovations come from what Nassim Taleb, author of *The Black Swan*, calls "positive black swans." While these innovation projects, Harford argues, do not have a known payoff or a fixed probability—in fact, no one ever really knows what ideas will work or even why—they cannot be predicted or planned. For this reason, their very existence depends upon our ability to vary our approach, even trying the opposite of what we might think will work, in service of research and development.[13]

Dialectical Thinking Leads to Multiple Perspectives

Variation *only* becomes possible when beliefs are not fixed and multiple perspectives are held. It is when we are willing to be open to new opportunities, try new approaches, and vary when needed. This is also why, as Harford points out, we don't look for innovation on isolated islands and that isolated ideas—those that are not subjected to the broad fitness landscape—do not lead to innovative concepts. The reason is that beliefs that are fixed—not subjected to contrary beliefs—offer little variance.

Innovation, whether it be in development or in reconsidering which areas of one's life to salvage and which ones to throw away after a setback, depends on varying one's approaches, holding multiple perspectives, accepting change as a constant state, and understanding that progress is not linear.[14]

While dialectical thinking might be considered "the greatest achievement of classical German philosophy"[15] and is a requirement of adaptation, it challenges everything we think of when it comes to solutions. When searching for solutions—particularly after setbacks, we naturally tend to ask the question, What is the best option? We tend to concentrate our efforts on one singular solution. And when that solution doesn't work, it's back to the drawing board to try another one. Trying multiple solutions—although it increases the chance of innovation, raises the survival probability from an evolutionary perspective, and ultimately leads to better outcomes—seems against our very instincts. Yet if thoughts cannot be flexible enough—viewpoints not able to be seen as both positive and negative—to allow for multiple, varied approaches, solutions that might work can easily be missed. To be sure, as Harford points out, physiological evolution—and the development of particular physical traits—does not follow a planned approach, and neither does the evolution of our thoughts.

Instead of throwing one dart, evolution throws multiple darts, and when it comes to cognitive evolution—rebuilding of fundamental beliefs after they have been shattered and rendered ineffective—maybe even at multiple targets. What people believe cannot often be distilled to one thing but rather a handful—in the case of Janoff Bulman, three core beliefs—aimed at achieving multiple goals.

Small Changes Lead to Big Changes

Yet dialectical thinking also asserts the idea that small changes (quantitative) lead to larger changes (qualitative). This is also what Harford would call "marginal changes" or focusing on the small improvements that, when combined, add up to a larger change. These marginal changes (Harford points to the seven gold medals won in 2012 by the British cycling team when Matt Parker focused on small changes in the team approach, such as avoiding the "pathogen-rich" Olympic bus, bringing pillows from home to ensure better rest, maximizing the one hour between the semifinals and the finals to get the best recovery, and using alcohol to clean the debris from the bike tires to gain better traction) are also how we recover from setbacks. Change is slow and hard to measure, but, over time, adds up. And it is often paradoxical. While we may be functioning better during the day, we may also continue to struggle with nightmares.

And yet, this again runs counter to how we treat distress symptoms, because what we are focusing on is the distress, asking questions like, Are you sleeping better? Having fewer flashbacks? Less anxiety? Is your mood improved? What we are missing are those small strength gains—marginal changes—that come from facing challenge. Maybe we have learned to accept that nothing is perfect and in turn become more accepting of ourselves and others. Maybe we have also learned that the world is both good and bad, and it is our subjective interpretation of the situation that ultimately grounds us and determines the way we feel. While these little changes are often missed while trying to mitigate what seems like larger problems—anxiety, flashbacks, nightmares, fear, and depression are not minor problems—they add up to larger change. Because what we are talking about is not just a refining of our thoughts, rebuilding our fundamental beliefs, we are talking about refining our skills and honing our strengths for the purpose of getting better at adapting. *And change is both slow and paradoxical.*

This is what Kevin, whom we met in chapter 1, discovered when, in cooking meals for the residents of the homeless shelter where he also lived, he found a passion. And while he could not afford a place to live and could not salvage the wreckage of his house or his business, he had made immeasurable gains in life satisfaction. It was, in fact, the first time in his life he had ever been truly happy. And yet he had lost everything. But on a more fundamental level, Kevin had learned that he could accept the paradox of his situation. That, in fact, it was accepting the paradox that brought tremendous happiness. There is, as Kevin stated, "a relief in not having to make everything perfect, in just accepting that some things are great, while others are really bad, and that's just life."

And this is what Sally, whom we also met in chapter 1, meant when she stated that her husband "really was a wonderful husband, even though he was clearly tortured and ultimately took his own life." She had learned to see things from multiple perspectives. He wasn't all bad as she'd initially thought, and yet, he wasn't the perfect man she thought she'd married. But what Sally, Kevin, and others like them had learned is not just to accept life's contradictions but to *use* them to dramatically improve happiness. That is, in understanding that progress and growth are paradoxical, there is more growth.

And change is an ongoing process. As Harford points out, what works for today might not work for tomorrow. Therefore, there are no qualities, traits, characteristics, or attributes that are either final or completely homogenous.

But what change does do is build upon itself. What Fichte called helical growth, Harford might refer to as improved feedback loops. What helical growth suggests and feedback loops provide—especially open ones—is the ability to examine our approach, measure our progress, and adapt. And while change is not circular—that is, improvements in *a* do not necessarily lead to improvements in *b*—the upward (helical) growth trend of dialectical thinking challenges us to redefine what we call growth. In this model, growth is not measured through the ability to implement a planned approach but rather the ability to adapt the approach to the feedback received. How well one processes and reads the landscape, adapts the plan, and again processes the feedback determines growth.[16]

And no time could the feedback be more profound—and sometimes unsettling—than after a setback. Yet in processing this, attempting to rebuild our beliefs and reconcile what we knew of ourselves, others, and the world with what we now know, the greatest advances in growth occur. Not surprisingly then, the more deeply and fundamentally our beliefs are challenged, the more considerable the growth. It is when experience defies everything we know to be true that we must come to terms with stark contradictions: that ourselves, others, and the world are not good or bad but rather a combination of both. But we also come to see that change is not measured in leaps and bounds but in the small steps we take toward a larger goal and our ability to see that progress is determined by our ability to adapt.

Four

The Gratitude Advantage

"Gratitude is not only the greatest of virtues,
but the parent of all others."

—Marcus Tullius Cicero

In his 2012 TED talk, Dan Gilbert, the author of *Stumbling on Happiness*, states, "A year after losing the use of their legs, and a year after winning the lotto, lottery winners and paraplegics are equally happy with their lives."

For most people this makes no sense. Why would it be that losing everything wouldn't fundamentally change our happiness levels? This is, after all, what most of us believe. It's why we try to avoid setbacks, mitigate losses, and improve our health. If having losses—and none might be so severe as the ones suffered by paraplegics—can mean that we arrive at the exact same place as when we win the lottery, why should we spend so much time trying to avoid them?

Maybe we shouldn't.

But we still need an answer. How is it possible that losing the use of limbs can lead to the same level of happiness as winning the lottery? And what does this mean about the way we look at setbacks? To answer these questions, we first have to consider two possibilities.

The first is that what we predict will make us happy doesn't. That is, in considering what leads to happiness, and making decisions based on happiness, we choose wrongly.

The second possibility is that *losing everything leads to a profound feeling of appreciation for what we have left, and this feeling of appreciation is highly linked to happiness.*

Let's consider the first possibility.

Gilbert, and many others like him, have shown repeatedly that the attachments we make to certain outcomes—whether it is winning the lottery, having a child, getting a raise, or losing everything—are often wrong.

And this may have a lot to do with our beliefs about happiness.

Happiness, for most people, is inextricably linked to beliefs about experiences.[1] If we believe that earning a college degree will lead to happiness, we pursue that. And if we are raised in a family that values athletic achievement, we go after that.

But we are also highly influenced by the environment. The fascinating research of Richard Thaler and Cass Sunstein, authors of *Nudge: Improving Decisions about Health, Wealth, and Happiness,* has shown that the environment influences us much more than we think, even in subtle ways. In one study, Thaler and Sunstein had subjects read a passage that was primed toward slowness (using words such as "old," "tired," "weak," and "retirement") or a passage that was primed toward speed (using words like "energetic," "lively," "young," and "children") and then measured the subjects' walking speed down the hall as they exited the research lab. Without having any idea what was being measured or to which study group they had been assigned, the subjects showed something fascinating: the ones who had been primed to walk faster did just that, while participants who had read the passage primed for slowness did indeed walk slower.[2]

Neither group had been told anything about walking slower or faster; they had simply been exposed to it through verbal priming.

So we can be primed to act in certain ways that are presumed to lead to happiness. It's why we go for the promotion. It's why we want the big house on the nice street, the luxury vehicle in the garage, and the vacation home in Vail. And like it or not, we are constantly exposed to messages that tell us what will lead to happiness. We are told what to buy, what to wear, what to eat and when to eat it, and where to vacation. Yet we are also told that if we don't jump on the opportunity now, the chance will be gone. The sale ends tonight, you have to buy now, and the sale only lasts so long. Making use of our fear of missing out, or what Gregg Easterbrook, author of *The Progress Paradox: How Life Gets Better while People Feel Worse*, calls "loss avoidance," marketers not only prime us, they prod us.[3]

So what do many of us do? We pursue that esteemed position—the one with the hefty salary—so we can buy the nice house, the new car, and the fancy vacation home. And the zest with which we go after this American dream—the one that promises happiness—can only be equated to a disease called "affluenza," according to John de Graaf, David Waan, Thomas Naylor, and David Horsey, authors of *Affluenza: The All-Consuming Epidemic.* What these authors cite is a multitude of unequivocal examples of all-out consumerism—in each of the past four years, more Americans declared personal bankruptcy than graduated from college, we have twice as many shopping centers as schools, and our annual production of solid waste would fill a convoy of garbage trucks stretching to the moon—that all lead to the same conclusion: *we have been led to believe that all this spending will bring us happiness.*[4]

Yet nothing could be further from the truth.

Consider the data presented by Easterbrook:

"The percentage of Americans who describe themselves as happy has not budged since the 1950s, though the typical person's real income more than doubled during that period. Happiness has not increased in Japan or Western Europe in the past half century either, though daily life in both of those places has grown fantastically better. Adjusting for population growth, unipolar depression, the condition in which a person simply feels blue, is ten times as prevalent as it was half a century ago."[5]

Easterbrook goes on to make the case that the way we link material wealth to happiness is a "nature's revenge law" where no matter how much money you have, there will always be something you can't afford. And while you will never be materially satisfied, you will also have "reference anxiety" because you will be comparing yourself to those around you and worrying that you are not keeping up. You will always be expecting more, and regardless of how high your income is, the minute it plateaus, so will your happiness.

Because the truth is, as Easterbrook accounts, "Most of what people really want in life—love, friendship, respect, family, standing, fun—is not priced and does not pass through the market. If something isn't priced, you can't buy it, so possessing money doesn't help much."

While this premise may seem obvious upon second glance, many of us fall for it. As one man described to me, "You just get stuck in a cycle where you know you are unhappy, you can't quite figure out why, so you just keep buying things trying to make yourself feel better. But at the end of the day, you are still stuck with yourself—and a lot of stuff you don't really need."

In terms of predicting what makes us happy, we often pursue a set of false beliefs about happiness—that is, that the things we think will make us happy actually don't. But when it comes to predicting our happiness, we also make another error: we miscalculate the impact that losses will have on us.[6]

Pointing to what is called the impact bias, Gilbert explains that when considering the future, and the way we will feel about the future, we tend to overestimate the hedonic impact of future events. The flip side of this, as Gilbert also mentions, is that we also tend to overestimate the negative impact of bad events.

Making his point, Gilbert quotes Moreese Bickham, who spent thirty-seven years in the Louisiana State Penitentiary for a crime he didn't commit. Upon being released, Bickham stated, "I don't have one minute's regret; it was a glorious experience."

No one would consider that such a fundamental loss would lead to happiness, and certainly not a "glorious experience," but the point to be made is that we make a profound miscalculation. And the miscalculation is not in whether or not losses will undermine our happiness—they will. *The real miscalculation we make is in our ability to adapt.*

Perhaps it's the unknown nature of losses that clouds our predictions, or perhaps it's that we have an innate ability to take the events that happen to us and "find a way," as Gilbert states. We don't see our own ability.

Yet here again, we might be more influenced by the environment than we would like to admit. Because while child psychologists tell us that all attempts to shape a child's behavior should employ the use of a three-to-one ratio—three positive statements to one bid for change (criticism)—we expose ourselves to something entirely different. Ray Williams, author of *Breaking Bad Habits*, reports that media studies show that bad news far outweighs good news by as much as seventeen negative news reports for every one good news report.[7]

The supposition that Williams makes is that the media exploits our own biological tendency to focus more—and be impacted more—by bad events than positive ones. And because, as we know from chapter 1, we seek to elaborate negatively charged emotions more than positive ones, we will return to the negative news again and again.

But there might be another reason we are saturated by negative news. Negative news keeps us feeling bad, and as the story goes, the way to happiness is to spend. The supposition is that the worse we feel, the more we will spend. Making matters worse, an anxious, depressed state does not lead to wise spending decisions.

And being made to feel negative—and primed to reach for a cure that cannot possibly make anyone feel better—in many ways, we are put into a state of learned helplessness. And while in this state, it's not surprising that when bad events do give us a feeling of helpless in our own lives, we miscalculate the way in which we will respond to them.

Now let's consider the second possibility.

The idea that losing everything somehow leads to actually feeling more grateful seems entirely foreign to most people. But as we already know, we make some pretty big mistakes when it comes to predicting how we will feel.

And losses have an undeniable effect on gratitude.

The reason they do is because, as Joseph and Linley (2005), two researchers who study losses and the processes we take to get through them, suggest, *gratitude is an essential part of the recovery process.* It appears that people's recovery from the traumatic experience is influenced by the extent to which they are able to find some benefit in the experience.[8] And the kinds of benefit people report—living life to the fullest, greater appreciation of family and friends, and valuing each day more.

Gratitude Orients Us to Notice The Positives

Whether it's valuing each day more, living life more fully, or simply appreciating those "little moments," gratitude has a remarkable effect on the way we get through any kind of adversity. Gratitude orients us toward noticing the positive aspects of our lives, which is especially helpful in light of losses.

In the words of one survivor, "even the smallest joys in life took on a special meaning."[9] These little moments of joy—a child's smile, spending time with loved ones, a beautiful sunset—add up to profound appreciation for what we still have.

Gratitude Alters Our Priorities

Gratitude, and especially the kind that comes from losses, changes our priorities. For many people who report severe life setbacks, the sense of being "so lucky" is not uncommon. And gratitude causes one to value what's left—just as Amy Purdy, the world's top-ranked Paralympic snowboarder, related after losing both legs to bacterial meningitis, "I almost lost my left hand and my nose—it could have been much worse."

To many of us, the story seems unbelievable. But Amy Purdy, in looking back upon her experience, "wouldn't change it." And Amy's experience isn't unique. Several trauma survivors also report "not wanting things to be different." In the words of one survivor, "This was the one thing that happened in my life that I needed to have happen, it was probably the best thing that ever happened to me."[10]

Gratitude Enhances Purpose

Losses, setbacks, and traumas put things in perspective. They cause us to take a look at how we were living—to acknowledge that life could have been lost—and to reconsider what is really important. This leads to a profound recalibration of values and a much more purposeful life. As one cancer survivor stated, "I don't concern myself with life's small inconveniences, and I don't have patience for chronic complainers. I am so grateful for having survived cancer...I'm living the best life I can, and I don't take anything for granted."[11]

The connection between gratitude and a purposeful life may explain what many have found when studying Vietnam War veterans. Those who reported higher levels of gratitude had more positive daily functioning (irrespective of symptomatology). But this might also be why a second study found a positive relationship between posttraumatic growth and recovery from trauma.[12]

The idea postulated by those who study posttraumatic growth is that trauma can lead to profound growth. That in going through even horrific experiences, there can be growth that surpasses pretrauma functioning. And some of the most undeniable evidence for posttraumatic growth can be found when looking at the September 11 attacks in 2001. Peterson and Seligman (2003) measured people before and after the attacks on the VIA inventory of psychological strengths, which acts as a map of positive functioning.[13, 14] Astoundingly, *gratitude was shown to increase over this period.*

And this was not the only study. Several subsequent studies showed that gratitude appeared to increase for both adults and children after the attacks.[15]

There is something about losses, even the most profound ones, that dramatically increases gratitude.

Gratitude has a Place in Evolution

Beyond simply making us feel better, gratitude may have an evolutionary place. Gratitude appears to be cross-culturally and linguistically universal and has been demonstrated repeatedly in the behavior of nonhuman primates—a handshake, for example, is a universal symbol of gratitude. Gratitude also appears to fill three prosocial needs: It is a benefit detector and both a reinforcer and motivator of prosocial behavior.[16]

Frans de Waal, best known for his research on morality in primates, cites the following example:

"Azalea, a trisomic rhesus macaque (trisomic = born with three copies of a certain chromosome), had abnormal motor and social skills, in ways somewhat akin to humans with Down syndrome. Instead of punishing her "incomprehensible blunders," such as threatening the alpha male, the other macaques were accepting and forgiving of her until Azalea's death at age three. Female chimpanzees may confront and shut down an overly aggressive male, sometimes even pulling two adversaries close together for reconciliation, or prying rocks from an aroused male's hands."[17]

The point de Waal makes is that even animals understand morality—and the evolutionary value of helping a partner, feeling gratitude, and returning the favor. He notes another 2011 study where chimpanzees given a free choice between helping only themselves or helping themselves plus a partner preferred the latter, and he went further to demonstrate the understanding of fairness and a desire for an equitable outcome in chimpanzees when playing the Ultimatum game. In this classic game, one player must decide how to split a sum of money between himself and another player whom he does not know. If the second player refuses the offer, both players receive nothing, and the game is only played once so reciprocity is not a factor. What de Waal showed was that chimpanzees respond in the same way as children and human adults—by preferring the equitable outcome.

Recent work on prosocial tendencies in apes and monkeys further supports de Waal's position. Felix Warneken, a psychologist at the Max Planck Institute for Evolutionary Anthropology in Leipzig, Germany, demonstrated that in a study on instrumental helping in human-reared chimpanzees, chimpanzees were found to help their caregiver when she was reaching for an object.[18] Considering the result was due to the fact that the chimpanzees had been raised by humans, Warneken tested the effect with chimpanzees that had been reared in the wild but had some exposure to humans—coming to a shelter daily for feeding—and found the same results.

Interestingly, the behavior of the chimps is not different from what has been witnessed in human infants in similar settings. In the words of Warneken:

"One major finding of this study was that, just like human infants tested in a similar situation, chimpanzees helped over consecutive trials by handing the out-of-reach object when the experimenter indicated that he was trying to get the object, and they did so irrespective of being rewarded."[19]

These observations, plus the adaptive value of cooperating with nonfamily members and sustaining reciprocal altruism, raise the possibility that gratitude evolved to facilitate social exchange.[20]

Social exchange depends on a sense of fairness, often called reciprocal altruism. Based on the principle that gratitude regulates the response to altruistic acts, reciprocal altruism is sensitive to the cost/benefit ratio of social acts. The theory goes that when someone does a favor for us, we feel grateful, weigh the cost of the act on the other person, and then return an act of similar weight. For example, when John offers to do the dishes, Sally responds with an offer to take out the trash.

But gratitude also encourages us to trust others, especially people we don't know so well. In an interesting study, researchers showed that gratitude increases people's trust in third parties, but only when they lack a high degree of familiarity with those third parties.[21] And again, this makes sense if survival is dependent on community effort, and what helps to convert acquaintance relationships into trusting ones is gratitude.

Gratitude may also have evolved to motivate not just returning acts of kindness to those who have been kind to us but also increasing the likelihood that we will "pay it forward." Known as "upstream reciprocity," passing gratitude's benefits on to third parties, instead of returning favors to one's benefactors, appears to be highly adaptive. In a sort of natural selection, when upstream reciprocity is present in a population that already exhibits reciprocal altruism—its members help one another—those who don't pay it forward tend to be weeded out. This effect was noted by de Waal when chimps were given a choice between a token that provided food for only themselves (selfish behavior) or a token that provided food for themselves and their partner (prosocial behavior). Interesting, chimps preferred the prosocial behavior—as much as three times as often as the selfish behavior—unless their partner was using pressure and intimidation tactics (in the case of chimpanzees, this equates to spitting water on the partner). When pressure and intimidation tactics were present, chimps' tendency to make prosocial choices dropped to almost baseline levels—no better than random. This selection pressure for gratitude is also what Nowak and Roch suggest—that gratitude is an intrinsic part of our nature.

Does Gratitude Make Us Happier?

While gratitude may have evolved to make us more cooperative, trusting, and favorable toward others, the question remains: Does this improve happiness?

Gratitude has been repeatedly linked to eudemonic well-being—the kind of purposeful, authentic living reported by trauma survivors.[22] And eudemonic well-being is highly related to happiness—in a longitudinal cohort of over 5,500 people initially aged fifty-five to fifty-six years, Wood and Joseph showed that people low in eudemonic well-being were 7.16 times more likely to meet criteria for clinical depression ten years later.[23]

Gratitude also relates to willingness to forgive, which is associated with the absence of psychopathological traits and is integral to positive functioning. Gratitude is connected to low narcissism and appears to strengthen relationships and promote relationship formation and maintenance. Relationship connection and satisfaction also appear to be highly linked to gratitude, and experimental evidence suggests that gratitude may promote conflict resolution and increase reciprocally helpful behavior.[24]

Gratitude appears to also have important health ramifications and is associated with a significantly lower risk of major depression, generalized anxiety disorder, phobia, nicotine dependence, alcohol dependence, and drug "abuse" or dependence. Additionally, feeling thankful has been related to a much lower risk of bulimia nervosa, which is not surprising given that interventions that increase gratitude appear to improve body image.[25]

Looking at the role of gratitude in staving off posttraumatic stress disorder, researchers looked at a sample of Vietnam War veterans, including forty-two patients diagnosed with PTSD and a control group of thirty-five comparison veterans, to find that gratitude is "substantially lower in people with PTSD." Further, gratitude was shown to relate to higher daily self-esteem and positive affect above the effects of symptomatology.[26]

Gratitude also appears to improve sleep. Many studies have specifically examined the possible relationships between gratitude and sleep in a community sample of 401 people, 40 percent of whom had clinically impaired sleep. Gratitude was related to total sleep quality, sleep duration (including both insufficient and excessive sleep), sleep latency (abnormally high time taken to fall asleep), subjective sleep quality, and daytime dysfunction (arising from insufficient sleep). In each case, gratitude was related to sleep through the mechanism of presleep cognitions. Negative thoughts prior to sleep are related to impaired sleep, whereas positive presleep cognitions are related to improved sleep quality and quantity.[27]

And gratitude appears to offer a buffer against negative emotions. In three separate studies, it has been negatively correlated with depression.[28] This is also consistent with the life orientation approach to gratitude, as being oriented toward the positive seems to counteract the "negative triad" of beliefs about self, world, and future seen in depression.[29]

The single measure of gratitude appears to be linked to more independent traits of well-being than any other measure. It has been correlated with positive emotional functioning, lower dysfunction, and positive social relationships. Grateful people score as less angry and hostile, depressed, and emotionally vulnerable, and experience positive emotions more frequently. Gratitude has also been correlated with traits associated with positive social functioning, emotional warmth, gregariousness, activity seeking, trust, altruism, and tender-mindedness. Finally, grateful people had higher openness to their feelings, ideas, and values, and greater competence, dutifulness, and achievement striving.[30]

When it comes to the way losses affect us, we make some pretty big miscalculations. Not only do we fail to consider that we are not the best predictors of our emotional states but more importantly, we profoundly underestimate our ability to adapt. *And when it comes to adapting—learning to leverage our losses in service of ultimate growth—we fail to see the advantage that gratitude offers.*

Five

Vulnerable Yet Stronger—

The Paradox of Strength

*"We are at our most powerful the moment
we no longer need to be powerful."*

—Eric Micha'el Leventhal

"No one ever gets through this life without heartache, without turmoil, and if you believe and have faith and you can get knocked down and get back up again and you believe in perseverance as a great human quality, you find your way." The words of Diana Nyad, the first swimmer to successfully swim the channel from Florida to Cuba, ring true.[1]

And yet so many of us try to minimize, avoid completely, and when everything else fails, deny that we have been knocked down. We try to turn away from the struggle to avoid the inevitable: everybody gets knocked down.

Why should we? Because what we are all trying to avoid is that one thing that no one wants to admit.

And that is vulnerability.

Yet there is no avoiding it. Setbacks, losses, and adversity simply makes us vulnerable—incredibly so.

And there are many reasons for this. The nature of the setback is one. If we perceive that our life, or the life of another, could have been lost, we also recognize how close we are, at all times, to losing a life.

If we have undergone stress, trauma, or hardship early on, we may be familiar with the feeling of powerlessness and the vulnerability that goes with it. And this will make us more likely to feel that way again. For many people, it is these early wounds that set forth a pattern of vulnerability that is not so easily unraveled.

Multiple stresses or setbacks also compound the feeling of vulnerability. When hardship and distress cannot be compartmentalized in one area of our lives, but instead bleed out across many domains of life, we are more likely to feel vulnerable.

And certainly, the closer to home the setback is, the more it hurts. Failures and losses that are a few degrees separated from us, and are not so closely tied to who we are, are much easier to take. This is why a grandchild misbehaving is not as unsettling as a child misbehaving. And this is also why things we are personally responsible for generate much greater feelings of shame and vulnerability when they don't go our way—because there is no one else to help shield the blame.

But setbacks don't have to be so severe to make us feel vulnerable. Because as Brene Brown, author of *Daring Greatly: How the Courage to Be Vulnerable Transforms the Way We Live, Love, Parent, and Lead,* describes, what ultimately underpins the feeling of vulnerability is shame.[2] And we feel shame any time we feel as though we are not accepted. Not accepted because the presentation was laughed at. Not accepted because we are from a different background. Not accepted because we are not as intelligent, pretty, thin, recognized, whatever, but somehow, just not enough.

And what we do, Brown explains, is develop shields to avoid the feeling of vulnerability. Because vulnerability is "exposure, uncertainty, and emotional risk," we learn that it is unsafe and it makes us appear stupid, unsure, and unprepared. Brown cites numerous examples of just how vulnerability is discouraged in business, society, and life.

Yet it might be that vulnerability isn't just discouraged from many external sources in our daily lives; perhaps we are instinctively wired to avoid it. In several interesting experiments studying the responses of poker players after losses, Tim Harford describes the erratic moves players make after losing a hand: "Acknowledging the loss and recalculating one's strategy would be the right thing to do, but that is too painful. Instead, the player makes crazy bets to rectify what he unconsciously believes is a temporary situation."[3]

Yet setbacks—and the vulnerability they lead to—are integral components of strength. Setbacks render us vulnerable and then call upon us to rise. And it is the struggle, the inherent uncertainty of a complex and novel problem with no easy answers, the failures along the way, the recognition of our weaknesses, and ultimately, our willingness to change course and adapt to the new circumstances that face us that develops strength.

Posttraumatic growth researchers describe this as the identification of strength being correlated, almost paradoxically, with an increased sense of vulnerability; they go on to say that growth is experienced as a combination of the knowledge that bad things can and do happen and the discovery that "if I handled this, I can handle just about anything."[4] Psychologists Richard Tedeschi and Lawrence Calhoun use the quote of a bereaved parent to further illustrate the transformative power of traumatic experience on the sense of personal strength: "I can handle things better. Things that used to be big deals aren't big deals to me anymore. Like big crisis problems, they will either work out or they won't. Whichever way it goes, you have to deal with it."[5]

And in recognizing the paradox—that strength is about being vulnerable and powerful—there is tremendous advantage.

Vulnerability Allows Us to Learn

The work of Carol Dweck, author of *Mindset: The New Psychology of Success*, has underscored the idea that in order to learn, children have to be able to become vulnerable—and admit failure. Dweck cites six separate studies where children are either praised for intelligence or hard work and then asked to choose between performance and learning goals for future problem-solving tasks. Dweck explains that

"children praised for intelligence after success chose problems that allowed them to continue to exhibit good performance (representing a performance goal), whereas children praised for hard work chose problems that promised increased learning. This finding was further supported by the interest that children showed in different types of information after they worked on the experimental tasks. Children praised for intelligence preferred to find out about the performance of others on the tasks rather than to learn about new strategies for solving the problems, even when these strategies might have improved their future performance. Children praised for effort, on the other hand, demonstrated their continued interest in mastery by preferring to receive strategy-related information. Thus, praise for intelligence seemed to teach children to value performance, even when following their own information-seeking interests, whereas praise for hard work seemed to lead children to value learning opportunities."[6, 7]

Interestingly, Dweck's findings tell us a lot more than just how feedback will affect learning strategies. What Dweck ultimately uncovered was that after facing failure, the children who had been praised for intelligence choose low-ability, rather than low-effort, attributions to account for their poor performance more than did children praised for hard work, who preferred to ascribe their failures to low effort. Essentially the kids who had been praised for hard work believed they failed because they hadn't worked hard enough, whereas the kids who had been praised for intelligence believed that they failed because they were not smart enough.[8, 9]

Not surprisingly, these attribution styles predicted how the kids behaved after setbacks as well. The kids who believed that lack of hard work was the cause of failure were not only more likely to work harder on subsequent trials, they also displayed more enjoyment of the task.

And they were much more likely to be honest. As Dweck recounts, "Children praised for intelligence showed a greater tendency to misrepresent their scores on the problems than did children praised for effort, in spite of the fact that their reports were anonymous and were not seen by the experimenter."[10] Again, not surprisingly, when failures and the learning that comes from acknowledging them are presented as things to be avoided, we tend to lie about them.

Dweck's work underscores the importance of allowing for exposure, shame, uncertainty, and emotional risk—all of those things that Brown notes cause us to avoid vulnerability—in the definition of learning. The problem was that when children were praised for intelligence, they associated it with something that is fixed—and they tended to avoid working harder after failures and even resorted to lying about them. And they showed significant distress after failures. On the other hand, when children were praised for hard work, they appeared to hold a more incremental theory of intelligence as malleable and to define intelligence in terms of motivation and knowledge. In essence, they were able to see that failures were a part of learning, and they were able to bounce back after them. In the words of Dweck, "These children did not appear to consider intelligence to be determined from any single performance and were found to avoid the postfailure achievement decrements of their intelligence praise counterparts."[11]

Developing what Dweck calls a "growth mind-set," when we see learning as an "active process" and one that allows us to be vulnerable, not only are we much more likely to try harder after setbacks, but we are much more likely to learn. In Dweck's studies, the children who had been praised for effort—and in which a growth mind-set was encouraged—raised their scores by an average of 30 percent on test trials. On the other hand, students who had been praised only for intelligence dropped their scores by nearly 20 percent. A big part of success, Dweck says, stems from our beliefs about what leads to success.[12]

Vulnerability Allows Us to Be Imperfect

Perfectionism is like a double-edged sword—a veritable duel with oneself in which failures, mistakes, and vulnerability are not acceptable. Known as "atelophobia," the symptoms of perfectionism are both emotional and physical.[13]

Emotions may be so overwhelming that we have difficulty thinking about anything other than the fear of failing. We may have feelings of disorientation or of being detached from ourselves. We tend to have a pessimistic view on the outcome of a situation before it happens, and we have extreme disappointment if we do fail. And not surprisingly, we also respond unrealistically—with exaggerated anxiety, anger, and jealously—when things don't go our way.

Physically, we can perspire due to stress, have nausea, dizziness, accelerated heart rate, chest pain, numbing, shortness of breath, muscle tension, and be locked in a constant state of restlessness.

Perfectionism, which Brown describes as the two-hundred-pound shield, is a self-destructive and addictive belief system. We think that if we are perfect, we can avoid or minimize the painful feelings of shame, judgment, and blame.

And having to be perfect is one strong reason we avoid vulnerability. The work of Dweck and her associates has demonstrated that children who hold performance goals—and have to be perfect to attain them—"are likely to sacrifice potentially valuable learning opportunities if these opportunities hold the risk of making errors and do not ensure immediate good performance."[14] These children tend to avoid "being challenged" in favor of "seeming smart."[15]

But having to be perfect doesn't just affect the choices we make when it comes to learning opportunities; it also predicts how we will respond to failures and setbacks. As Dweck explains, "an emphasis on performance goals has been linked to vulnerability to a maladaptive helpless response to achievement setbacks, which is characterized by negative affect, negative self-cognitions, and performance impairment in the face of failure."[16]

Vulnerability allows us to be imperfect, to choose learning over performance, to choose growth over stagnancy, and ultimately, to choose a proactive response over helplessness in the face of setbacks.

Vulnerability Allows Us to Take Risks

Being uncertain is one reason we avoid vulnerability, but it is also a major reason we avoid risk. If we can't be allowed to be uncertain of the outcome, we will be locked into a predicted path and will not adapt when circumstances call for it, like after we experience a setback.

Avoiding risk, according to Harford, is a recipe for failure. Being willing to take a risk, as Harford explains, allows us to try new things, which, he notes, is exactly what we have to do when facing a setback. But being willing to take a risk also means we are willing to fail.

And failing, according to Harford, is one of the core components of success.[17] As Harford explains, when describing "skunk works operations"—those that are allowed to fail—there "is no guarantee of success in the face of disruptive innovations." What skunk works do allow us to do, however, is be uncertain, vary our approach, take chances, and risk failure. Ultimately these variations in approach offer that shot at success—even if it is against the odds.

Interestingly, vulnerability may also protect us from taking risks that are too great. When summarizing the behavior of chess players after losses, the two prominent behavioral psychologists Daniel Kahneman and Amos Tversky explain that "making peace with losses," which requires vulnerability, seems to stave off the tendency to take wild gambles after losing. Kahneman and Tversky's observations are seconded by Harford, who notes that "chasing our losses" in an attempt to avoid accepting them and thereby taking erratic risks to recover from them is common among players of the popular game show *Deal or No Deal.* In the show, contestants begin with an unknown prize in a box and are given the opportunity to trade their box for a different one—also with an unknown prize amount. They are periodically offered the ability to "deal" and accept a monetary offer instead of accepting their own box. What the show uncovers is how people handle risks—particularly after making unlucky choices. Richard Thaler, the noted behavioral economist who studied contestants, found that *after making unlucky choices, participants were much more likely to refuse the monetary offer—the safer and better bet—and continue playing while taking greater risks.* This effect is especially striking given that the monetary offers made to the contestants who made unlucky choices were much more generous than those made to the contestants who had made lucky choices.[18]

Yet if we can accept the losses (as Rob, whom we met in chapter 1, says about being fired from his teaching job when it was discovered that he was gay, "I've already been through the worst; what else did I have to lose?"), and if we don't fear vulnerability, we are also able to take the important risks that developing strength depends on. For Rob this equated to putting all of his savings into a new Internet company and facing the uncertainty that comes with risking everything with only the hope of success somewhere in the distance.

It seems that vulnerability allows us to calculate our risks—to find the important middle ground between fixed patterns that do not allow for adaptation and erratic chances—and take them because they will lead to growth.

Vulnerability has an Evolutionary Advantage

Aside from the advantages vulnerability may have for learning, there is evidence that it also has significant adaptive advantages. As Brown states, "vulnerability is the birthplace of empathy."

Witnessing a person in a vulnerable state enacts what is known as a negative-state relief model of response—where our motives for helping them stem from the personal distress we feel when exposed to their plight.[19] The empathy that comes from identifying with another person and feeling and understanding what that person is experiencing leads to the innate tendency to help him or her.[20, 21]

And this decision to help, according to the empathy-altruism hypothesis by Daniel Batson, depends *primarily* on whether we feel empathy for the person. Batson goes on to argue that pure altruism is motivated by the empathy that we feel for the person in need; that is, when we are able to experience events and emotions the way that that person experiences them.[22]

And when we know someone is in a vulnerable state, we are much more likely to feel empathy and, ultimately, are more likely to help. One study found that those high in empathy were much more likely to help a fellow student who had ostensibly broken both legs in an accident and was behind in classes.[23]

A separate study showed similar results. Researchers divided participants into a high-empathy group and a low-empathy group. They both had to listen to another student, Janet, who reported feeling lonely. The study found that the high-empathy group (told to imagine vividly how Janet felt) volunteered to spend more time with Janet, whether or not their help was anonymous, which makes the social reward lower.[24] This study points to the role of empathy in motivating helping behavior—regardless of the cost and reward.

And vulnerability may influence more than just the decision to help. While we can recall from chapter 4 and de Waal's trisomic rhesus macaque, Azalea, that primates will come to the aid of another with increased frequency when witnessing that one in a vulnerable state, the work of Robert Sapolsky suggests another evolutionary purpose for vulnerability. Measuring glucocorticoid levels, which are an indication of stress, in wild baboons living in a national park in Kenya, Sapolsky notes that when under stress, such as being a low-ranking member of a group or when the dominance hierarchy of that group is unstable, it's the baboons who have higher levels of social support (in Sapolsky's experiments, this equates to fellow group members coming to the aid of members in distress) that have lower levels of glucocorticoids.[25] And these group members come to their aid *because* they are vulnerable.

The work of both de Waal and Sapolsky suggests that vulnerability and empathy both have important adaptive purposes. Vulnerability enhances connection because it creates a physiological response, a distress signal that we feel when witnessing the suffering of another. And when we feel what another feels, what we know as empathy, we are instinctively compelled to help. Yet the help that vulnerability elicits does much more than connect us. Receiving social supports helps us cope with stress.

While Sapolsky originally noticed this effect in wild baboons, he notes that "this can be demonstrated even in transient instances of support. In a number of subtle studies, subjects were exposed to a stressor such as having to give a public speech or perform a mental arithmetic task, or having two strangers argue with them, with or without a supportive friend present. In each case, social support translated into less of a cardiovascular stress-response."[26]

Vulnerability Helps Us Cope

The effects of social support go beyond the physiological markers of stress Sapolsky noticed in his baboons. Studying survivors of major life traumas, Tedeschi and Calhoun found that the ability to disclose to supportive others was a key component in coping. What cognitive disclosure allows survivors to do, Tedeschi and Calhoun note, is to retell their story, ease emotionally charged material, and craft new life narratives that support positive adaptation after traumatic events. Other researchers identify positive adaptation after traumatic events as *dependent* on disclosure—to supportive others—and suggest that "failure to confide in others about traumatic events is associated with increased incidence of stress-related disease."[27] And disclosure—especially of emotionally charged material—puts us in a vulnerable state. Yet in order to reap the rewards of social support, we must be willing to be vulnerable.

Vulnerability, when it is displayed in the distress of another, enacts the feeling of empathy for that person and the desire to help.[28] Vulnerability connects us, and social disclosure depends on it. But more than anything, vulnerability is a crucial component in the development of personal strength. Because at no time is strength tested more than when coping with challenges—when we are in the thick of the struggle—and vulnerability brings with it the critical empathy and help from others. Vulnerability is the backbone of social disclosure, which is what we need to develop the kind of strength necessary to reveal ourselves, to reflect upon our responses, and to ultimately adapt to our changed circumstances and create a new life narrative when we are most challenged.

The case can certainly be made that vulnerability aids learning, allows for the imperfections and risks necessary to adapt to the changing circumstances after a setback, and that it has an adaptive purpose. There is perhaps no better evidence for the role vulnerability has in the definition of strength than when looking to studies of posttraumatic growth.

For many it is surprising enough that growth can occur after what many of us would consider insurmountable losses, but what is even more astounding is that the work of several researchers points to the conclusion that *the more beliefs are challenged by a traumatic event, the more growth will emerge.*[29]

Studying the behavior of people after tremendous losses, these researchers found not just that greater losses lead to greater strength gains, but that growth and distress often coexist. *That is to say that distress, feeling vulnerable, occurs along with profound gains in strength.*

Even further, the research of Tedeschi and Calhoun suggests that the longer the complications of the trauma persist, the greater the gains in growth. In what they identify as "greater cognitive engagement" in attempting to process the trauma, we can also identify a longer learning curve.[30] That is to say, the longer and more complicated the battle—and the more formidable our opponent—the more adept a warrior we will become.

It is when the answers do not come easily that our greatest gains in strength occur. As Sara, whom we met in chapter 2, states, "I had to fight for what I have, but I also finally realized I could fight."

Almost in direct relationship, the more completely we are challenged, the greater the opportunity we have for growth. But growth also depends on our ability to be vulnerable, to make mistakes, to be willing to fail, to be uncertain and take risks, and to adapt our approach—for this is how we get stronger. And in no case can this be more important than when facing setbacks.

Six

Connection—What We Crave the Most

*"We're never so vulnerable than when we trust
someone—but paradoxically, if we cannot
trust, neither can we find love or joy."*

—Frank Crane

When faced with life events that bring depressive, traumatic, and socially inappropriate thoughts to the fore, the most common strategy is the avoidance of those thoughts.[1]

Setbacks, by their very nature, bring a tremendous amount of distress. When things don't go as we want, there are a number of ways we can feel about it—inferior, unloved, invisible, unaccepted, inadequate, humiliated, undeserving, weak, guilty, discarded, and dishonored.

And naturally, we all have different ways of managing these feelings. Most people, however, employ avoidance—simply focusing on information that is relevant to the truth they want to believe and filtering out any evidence to the contrary. What we know from chapter 2 is that cognitive biases are common to all people in all situations—*and certainly when faced with adversity.*

But denial is not just a phenomenon supported by cognitive biases; it's also how we cope with distress. Sometimes it serves us, as Sara, whom we met in chapter 2, said after being in a mass theatre shooting: "It was just easier to go to work the next day and pretend it was a normal day." Sometimes avoidance is what we need to do to keep functioning.

So we suppress thoughts, avoid people, places, even images that remind us of the harmful events. We pretend we are OK. And we avoid talking about it.

Because for most people, like Sara, the idea of discussing a hurtful past is associated with "reliving it," complete with all of the negative emotions. The idea is that disclosing the details of a trauma, setback, or failure will mean *being right there again, feeling the same feelings that were felt at that time.*

This is why Sara initially avoided talking about the horrific theatre shooting she endured, and when she did, she left out very pertinent details, like hiding under the seat in the theatre and not being sure her husband was still alive. This is also why Sally, whom we met in chapter 1, took several years to tell a single person the full details of her husband's suicide.

For both women, avoiding the vulnerability, shame, and fear associated with the events of their past was not just instinctive; it was indicative of a much larger and more profound fear: that their emotions would be so powerful that *they would lose control.* They were afraid that the sadness, fear, uncertainty, confusion—all things we feel with setbacks—would simply overwhelm their emotional capacity, and they would no longer be able to function.

The story that Sally told me, which she believed for many years, was that telling anyone about her husband's suicide and having to talk about it "would open up feelings that I just couldn't cope with, and I wouldn't be able to get out of bed the next day."

And some people, like Sara, learn to avoid vulnerability from early on—not letting anyone know how terrified she really was that night, that she hadn't been able to sleep through the night since, that she was constantly looking over her shoulder, and that she was afraid to leave the house—and associate it with weakness.

The fear of appearing weak, according to Leon F. Seltzer, PhD, who holds doctorates in English and psychology and is a clinical psychologist and author of *Paradoxical Strategies in Psychotherapy*, is a common reason we avoid talking about things that cause distress. As Seltzer states,

"Perhaps paramount among our tendencies to conceal our emotional fragility from others is the fear that exposing it would make us look weak to them—and, indeed, make us feel weak and powerless ourselves. We assume that frankly disclosing our hurt feelings would betray our susceptibility to them—and thus define ourselves as "one down" in the relationship, with all that might imply about placing them in a position to exploit us, or take advantage of us. It's as though in "exhibiting" our hurt we're forfeiting our personal power, relinquishing it to them to use over us in any way they deem fit."[2]

The point that Seltzer makes is not just that we are afraid of looking weak; it's that we are afraid of the social ramifications. *For people who avoid vulnerability, the real problem is trust.*

It's the ability to show your hand, let down your guard, leave yourself wide open, and trust that the person you are with will not take advantage of you. As Seltzer notes,

"The bottom line here is that we don't trust that others (or our "significant" other) will—by responding to our open-heartedness in caring, supportive ways—safeguard or validate our vulnerability.

Additionally, we may not trust ourselves to successfully cope with their response, whatever it is. And, assuming we're in self-protective mode, we're certainly not going to offer them the opportunity to make us feel any worse than we may already be feeling."[3]

And for people like Sara, who have had their trust broken—in her case, her mother told her to "stop acting like a baby; no one is going to rescue you," every time she cried—*the compulsion to avoid the experience again serves the instinct to avoid vulnerability.*

But there is another, perhaps even stronger, message people who avoid vulnerability learn. And that is *to avoid needing.* Because needing people can mean that they will disappoint you, they will let you down, and you will be hurt. Therefore, the way to avoid pain is to avoid having needs. And so these people, like Sara, become very strong warrior types who face challenge head on and don't admit they are afraid, scared, hurt, or in need. They simply learn to shut down the need for connection.

Interestingly, people such as this may also be afraid to *receive* compassion if the memory of compassion is associated with fear, pain, abuse, and shame. Many studies conducted with patients in therapy reflect the idea that some patients find it overwhelming to be self-compassionate and receive compassion from others, like a therapist, since the experience of these feelings in therapy may reactivate emotional memories of being shamed by an attachment figure, which then triggers conditioned emotional responses.[4, 5] Hence, feelings of warmth can be frightening and strange for these individuals and lead to anxiety, avoidance, aggression, or dissociation.

In Sara's case, coming to therapy and reaching out for help ignited the anger she felt first toward her husband, who was in many ways similar to her mother, and then at her mother for ignoring her requests for connection, which is what crying is for a child.

But this is also why setbacks that come from those close to us can have such a profound effect on our ability to connect with others. What these figures represent, as we discussed in chapter 2, are *models for how to operate in the world*. Sara's model, like many people's, simply told her to avoid connection—that connection was associated with pain, hurt, and rejection. Ultimately, that connection was associated with a lack of compassion.

And certainly for people whose close connection figures don't just ignore the need for connection but violate it, the case can be much worse. Jennifer Freyd, editor of the *Journal of Trauma and Dissociation*, developed what is known as the betrayal trauma theory to explain what happens when those close to us betray our trust. As Freyd notes,

"whereas victims of trauma perpetrated by a stranger may be motivated to either fight back or run away, these responses are less helpful in the case of betrayal trauma, in which the perpetrator is providing food, shelter, and/or emotional connection to the victim. It is also possible that feeling ashamed of oneself plays a protective function in close relationships characterized by abuse. For example, if a parent emotionally, physically, or sexually assaults a child, the child may feel ashamed of herself instead of feeling angry at or afraid of the abuser. Researchers such as Dacher Keltner have found that whereas anger often results in fighting and fear often results in fleeing, shame tends to result in submitting and appeasing. Thus, the expression of shame has the potential to elicit a caregiving response from the perpetrator, which could ultimately keep the victim as safe as possible within an unsafe situation."[6]

Paul Gilbert, author of *Shame: Interpersonal Behavior, Psychopathology and Culture*, seconds Freyd's assertion that shame has a protective mechanism and explains that it serves an adaptive purpose—to decrease the risk of future harm. According to Gilbert, "the expression of shame seems to use similar bio-behavioral systems to those of animals expressing submissive behaviors."[7]

Shame simply becomes what we do to stay safe. Feeling shame, in a betrayal system, helps us avoid physical harm, and in a system where connection has broken down, it helps us avoid emotional harm.

In either case, what is ultimately avoided is connection.

And at no time is connection more important than after a setback.

For those who study resolution of traumatic experience—what we now know as posttraumatic growth—connection, through the presence of supportive relationships and our ability to disclose, is how we make sense of setbacks of all kinds. Connection offers the opportunity to revisit compassion—reconsidering our "working models" for how others will respond to our vulnerability, and more deeply, our working models for how to trust.[8, 9, 10]

Connection Teaches Trust

The reason connection becomes so important after a setback is because learning how to trust is how we begin to process the setback. Researchers of adaptation to trauma, such as cancer diagnosis and treatment, suggest that the cognitive and emotional processing of traumatic experience that occurs through the disclosure and resultant "working through" of traumatic material leads to better adjustment.[11]

Disclosure is also how we begin to recreate a new narrative—the story that we tell ourselves about the setback—and this occurs through the incorporation of perspectives of others who have also been through similar traumas. These narratives become especially important after setbacks because, as we know from chapter 1, what setbacks do is fundamentally challenge our understanding of the world and cause us to reconsider questions of meaning, purpose, and, certainly, connection. In Sally's case, recrafting her narrative was the difference between telling herself,

"I am crazy for feeling this way, and no one can ever know what goes through my head because they will think I'm crazy," and "What I feel is a normal response, and actually, looking back, I can see how strong I am, even if I am also feeling more vulnerable." On a more fundamental level, disclosing her story, for Sally, was not just an incredible challenge to her ability to trust but also a profound way to deepen it.

Connection Restores Intimacy

Disclosure offers the restoration of intimacy, trust, and connection, and the opportunity to deepen these things. Because setbacks cause us to face our mistrust, which may or may not have been hidden from us, they force us to overcome it in order to ultimately reconfigure our reality, our understanding of the world, and our understanding of connection. Setbacks not just reaffirm the importance of deep, meaningful relationships but make us work for them.

For Kevin, whom we met in chapter 1, it wasn't until he lost everything that he became so acutely aware of his need to "have it all figured out" and his avoidance of uncertainty. It simply wasn't OK to admit that he didn't know and didn't have a plan. And yet his reality, when living in a homeless shelter, having lost his medical practice, house, and fiancée, was that he didn't have any idea what to do. To admit this to me was to challenge his fear that he would appear inadequate, and that his inadequacy would be used against him. In Kevin's words, "I thought that you would think I'm a total idiot. Here I am a doctor, living in a homeless shelter. I must look like an idiot."

From the example above, it's clear that connection doesn't just offer a feeling of comfort from someone who has "been there" and ease disclosure of uniquely charged emotional material but that setbacks themselves challenge the very understanding of relationships and force a *schema change about the relationship.* According to the International Society for Traumatic Stress Studies,

"Surviving a traumatic event may alter an individual's sense of safety and trust in ways that spill over into new or old relationships. Survivors may feel vulnerable and confused about who or what is safe. People who were rarely irritable in the past may display anger outbursts and hostile behaviors due to an increased sense of vulnerability and fear, both of which are heightened after a trauma. Survivors may also find it difficult to trust others, even people they trusted in the past. It may feel frightening to get close to people for fear of being hurt again. Trauma survivors might also feel angry at their helplessness and sense of loss of control in their lives. They may become aggressive or demanding, or try to control others as a way of regaining control."[12]

◆ ◆ ◆

Setbacks Make Connection Vital

The paradoxical nature of connection is brought to light through setbacks. On the one hand, setbacks make us feel more vulnerable, unsure, and fearful in relationships, yet on the other hand, in order to process them and begin the work of healing, we must trust—and at a much deeper level. Ultimately, setbacks challenge us to an increased sense of vulnerability and an increased sense of trust—in a sense, to experience connection more deeply and more authentically.

A quote from a bereaved parent exemplifies the shift in connection brought about by a major setback: "When he died, people just came out of the woodwork…I realize that relationships with people are really important now…and I cherish my husband a lot more."[13]

The words of another trauma survivor, quoted by Tedeschi and Calhoun, perhaps describe best how setbacks can clarify connection: "You find out who your real friends are in a situation like this."

In a sense, setbacks apply an almost Darwinian theory to relationships, where, in this "survival of the fittest," the relationships that survive are the ones that can tolerate an increased level of vulnerability, trust, and connection. And in the same way evolution refines traits that do not have an adaptive purpose and may jeopardize survival, some relationships will not survive setbacks. In fact, there will be a culling of the ones that do not. As Rob, whom we met in chapter 1, told me, "Some friends you realize are not really friends at all."

And applying an evolutionary theory to connection might not be the worst thing if it causes us to confront our fears, vulnerability, shame, and mistrust for the purpose of strengthening connection and along the way eliminating the relationships that jeopardize our survival.

We are Wired To Connect

In looking at the impact of connective mechanisms developed through social grooming in adult female baboons, Dunbar, an acclaimed primatologist, found three purposes. *First, social grooming provided a basis for protective alliances.* As Dunbar noted, "Among wild gelada baboons (*Theropithecus gelada*), the likelihood of a female going to the aid of another female when the latter is under attack is significantly correlated with the amount of time the two of them spend grooming with each other."[14] Additionally, more dominant animals are less likely to attack or harass an individual who is known to have grooming partners who might come to its aid.

Second, social grooming was linked to reproductive success. Dunbar measured the reproductive success (indexed as the number of surviving infants produced) of wild female savannah baboons (*Papio hamadryas cynocephalus*) to find it correlated with the number and intensity of their relationships (which, of course, are established and serviced by grooming).[15]

Lastly, connection supports attachment bonding. Dunbar found that adult female gelada support the progressive feeding-time demands of child rearing by sacrificing resting time, conserving their social time for as long as possible.[16]

But beyond the protective survival factors related to social grooming, or even the functional aspects—some researchers suggest that grooming occurs as part of a "market commodity" where grooming is traded for other favors, such as coming to one's aid when attacked by another dominant group member—there is a much deeper reason that primates spend so much time on grooming and developing the connection that comes with it. Grooming "creates a psychological environment of trust." Dunbar goes further to argue that trust is developed through "triggering a cascade of neuroendocrines," such as endorphins, endogenous opiates, oxytocin, and vasopressin.[17]

An association between grooming and endorphin release was demonstrated experimentally in talopin monkeys.[18] Dunbar also found a correlation between grooming and endogenous opiate levels. As Dunbar notes, "In effect, animals given opiate blockade appeared not to be able to get enough grooming, whereas those given opiates acted as if they were satiated and were disinterested in either giving or receiving grooming."[19]

And it appears that these neuropeptides come with a host of benefits.

Endorphins, or more generally endogenous opioids, play a well-understood role as part of the mechanisms of pain control.[20] Psychologically, this is experienced as a mild opiate "high," a corresponding feeling of well-being, and light analgesia.[21, 22, 23]

Oxytocin and vasopressin are closely related neuropeptides that seem to play a role in the processes of pair-bonding in mammals.[24, 25, 26, 27, 28, 29, 30, 31] Oxytocin also plays a role in ameliorating stress. One study showed that female oxytocin-deficient mice were more nervous in novel environments and had higher stress levels (indexed by corticosterone titres) in response to environmental stressors than did wild-type mice and that these symptoms could be alleviated by injecting oxytocin directly into the cerebral ventricles.[32] In rats, high doses of oxytocin give rise to a sedative-like effect, including lowered blood pressure and reduced locomotion.[33, 34, 35]

Connection matters, not just from an emotional perspective (facilitating vital disclosure of distressing material) but from a physiological perspective (creating an environment of trust).

Setbacks make connection relevant. They make connection matter. But they also remind us that connection is two things: It is fear inducing, and it is necessary. At no time are we more wary of connecting than after a setback, and at no time does connection become more important. And it is in this struggle—to find trust when it seems impossible, to weed out whom we can trust and whom we cannot, and to come face to face with our shame, humiliation, inadequacy, and rejection—that setbacks ultimately develop one of our greatest strengths.

Seven

FAITH—WHY IT MATTERS

*"Faith consists in believing when it is beyond
the power of reason to believe."*

—VOLTAIRE

For most people, faith is unclear. Just the word "God" invokes a variety of reactions. For one thing, some people don't believe God exists. And for those who do believe in God, the picture of just what it/he/she is can be quite different.

Yet, irrespective of any beliefs a person may have, faith requires belief in something that cannot be seen, reasonably sensed, felt, or evidenced in any clear way.

On the face of it, we simply have no rational reason to believe. And for many people, the faith question might be left right there—discarded as something not really worth pondering.

That is, until life events mimic the faith question. Setbacks, in many ways, can be just like pondering whether God exists, because when life deals us a major blow, it's hard to see how getting through is, in any way, possible. We can't see the way, we don't feel like we can go on, and we may not even be able to picture what going on looks like. The first steps we do take will be just like our first venture into faith; we will have to believe in something that rational conjecture doesn't support. We will have to trust that making it through is possible, even though it doesn't seem possible. And we might even have to believe in something larger than ourselves.

Ultimately, we will have to question our faith. But as it turns out, thinking about God has many benefits—especially in the face of setbacks. The fascinating research of noted neuroscientists Andrew Newberg, MD, and Mark Robert Waldman, authors of *How God Changes Your Brain: Breakthrough Findings from a Leading Neuroscientist,* shows that when we think about God, whether we focus on a visual representation or a cognitive description, several things happen to our brain. They relate the following conclusions:

- Each part of the brain constructs a different perception of God.
- Every human brain assembles its perceptions of God in uniquely different ways, thus giving God different qualities of meaning and value.
- Spiritual practices, even when stripped of religious beliefs, enhance the neural functioning of the brain in ways that improve physical and emotional health.
- Intense, long-term contemplation of God and other spiritual values appears to permanently change the structure of those parts of the brain that control our moods, give rise to our conscious notions of self, and shape our sensory perceptions of the world.
- Contemplative practices strengthen a specific neurological circuit that generates peacefulness, social awareness, and compassion for others.[1]

While Newberg and Waldman's findings might suggest that the benefits of faith revolve around the belief in God, evidence is widespread that a variety of spiritual practices including mediation, chanting, visualization, conscious repetition of phrases or visual images, and prayer produce tangible effects across many domains of life.[2] Neurological patterns begin to shift, allowing for a calmer, more focused brain; cognitive changes support enhanced engagement in solving complex and novel problems; mood is elevated; and perception and relation to others improves—all of which become crucial when challenged with a setback.

Faith Enhances Neural Function

Newberg and Waldman relate the results of a recent twelve-week study where various yoga practices were used to measure the effect on the brain. What these researchers found was that after twelve weeks, all participants tested with lowered activity in the amygdala, the part of the brain associated with anxiety. Further, mindfulness-based meditation, such as consciously labeling one's moment-to-moment feelings, also lowers amygdala activity.[3]

Looking at the data another way, several studies have indicated that injuries to the occipital cortex and the temporal lobes, which are associated with envisioning God and "listening to God's voice," can result in phenomena associated with mystical, religious, or demonic experience.

Meditation also appears to enhance parietal lobe activity, which regulates one's sense of self in relation to others, thereby improving relationships and the ability to resonate with others' thoughts and feelings.

The thalamus—the part of the brain that acts as the center of sensory processing, relaying sensations, thoughts, and moods to other parts of the brain—also appears to be enhanced through prayer and meditation. In their review of subjects who had meditated for over ten years, Newberg and Waldman found asymmetric activity between the right and the left half of the thalamus when these subjects were not meditating. While the general population typically shows equal activity on both sides of the thalamus, the asymmetric activity of meditators appeared to reveal an adaptation to repeated and consistent meditating on a thought. That is, over time, the brain begins to respond to the thought in the same way that it responds to sensations and moods that accompany the thought. In a way, meditating on something causes it to be neurologically real, as patterns in the brain shift much as they do during actual experience.

Neurotransmitters, which affect mood—chemicals such as dopamine, epinephrine, and serotonin—are also affected by spiritual practice. Dopamine, for example, which generates pleasurable experiences, is linked with reward, and stimulates positive thoughts, was shown to increase by 65 percent when individuals practiced yoga nidra, a form of meditation in which a person maintains conscious awareness while remaining in a state of complete relaxation.[4] Serotonin, which is linked to positive-affect states, a feeling of satiety, and general well-being, has also been shown to increase with spiritual practice. Gamma-aminobutric acid (GABA), which is associated with lower levels of depression and anxiety, can be increased by as much as 27 percent through gentle forms of yoga that involve breathing and stretching.[5] Transcendental Meditation—a combination of relaxation, breathing, and repeating a symbolic sound—has also been shown to lower stress molecules epinephrine and norepinephrine.[6]

Meditation and Visualization Improve Brain Function

Meditating on a single thought or idea has been linked to a host of benefits. Similar to visualization exercises used by athletes, when thoughts and statements are repeated frequently, they take on a neurological reality.

Much of the work of Martin Seligman, well recognized as the father of positive psychology and the author of *Learned Optimism,* has centered on the thoughts that we generate to explain events to ourselves. Known as attributions, these thoughts create neurological patterns in the brain. Negative attributions—such as "I am such a loser," "Things never work out," and "I always fail"—lead to lower levels of serotonin and higher levels of epinephrine. The result of this neurological cascade is a depressed mood and higher levels of anxiety. Positive attributions, on the other hand, show just the opposite response and are positively correlated with increased subjective measures of well-being.[7]

Neurological patterns are not the only things that change with conscious repetition. A study recently released by the Psychiatric Neuroimaging Research Program at Massachusetts General Hospital demonstrated that meditation enhanced the brain's thickness and neuroplasticity, which normally thins as we age.[8] Putting things simply, meditation improves the health of the brain, and the more specific the meditation, the more specific the response.

Wondering about just how this effect takes place, Richard Davidson, head of the Waisman Laboratory for Functional Brain Imaging and Behavior at the University of Wisconsin, studied long-term meditators to measure the brain's responses after thinking about a series of images or thoughts. He found that advanced meditators have the extraordinary ability to manipulate specific parts of the brain that control thoughts and emotions.[9] It appeared that after consciously focusing on images or thoughts linked to positive mood, such as the picture of a loved one, meditators could activate the same parts of their brain as when that person or object was experienced in reality.

This research seconds that done by many prominent sport psychologists that demonstrate that the same neuromuscular patterns involved in an activity can be activated by continuous imagery of the activity. And the results appear to play out on the field, as those athletes who consistently used imagery improved their game. One experiment separated volleyball players into high- and low-imaging groups and then further separated each group into novice and experimental groups. Regardless of the skill level of the player, high-visual-imagery groups showed significantly more improvement than the low-imagery group.[10] Another study went further to show that targeted imagery exercises created measurable autonomic nervous system (ANS) responses where those who used imagery elicited a specific ANS response related to the task they were visualizing. And the result yielded performance gains where those who used visualization improved performance. In light of this experiment, it was suggested that mental imagery "may help in the construction of schema which can be reproduced, without thinking, in actual practice."[11]

Imagery and visual rehearsal also appear to improve our desire to take on a challenging task. Using a sample of golfers, a 1995 study demonstrated that those who used visualization "had more realistic self-expectation, set higher goals to achieve, and adhered more to their training programs outside the experimental setting."[12]

Faith Improves Mood

The act of believing in something greater than oneself has been linked to a multitude of treatment modalities for everything from addiction to mood disorders. Meditation, for one, has been referenced often in the treatment of a variety of psychiatric disorders and has proven especially effective with severe depression.[13] Alcoholics Anonymous also makes use of spirituality and devotes an entire step of the twelve-step process to "giving oneself over to a higher power."

Additionally, the way in which spirituality directs attention to something larger than the self is especially helpful as those with distressing symptoms often focus only on the symptoms. In this way, spiritual practice broadens life's meaning to something beyond the suffering brought about by unsettling emotions. And suffering is also put in context by spirituality, as many religions connect sacrifice with enlightenment.

In looking at the way in which spiritual practice improves mood, Stephanie Pappas (writing for LiveScience) quoted Todd Kashdan, a psychologist at George Mason University, "We find that having a really spiritual day, committing to a power higher than yourself, carefully considering a purpose larger than yourself, it ends up leading to a lot of well-being." Kashdan went on to say, "We find profound levels of meaning in life, greater positive emotions, less negative emotions, higher self-esteem."[14]

It also seems to be that spirituality gives people a sense of meaning in life. Simply the acknowledgment of a greater purpose appears to be highly linked to an increased sense of life meaning and a deeper purpose for life beyond oneself. For this reason, spirituality has been especially useful during times of crisis when life events challenge meaning and purpose.

Faith Enhances Physical Health

A central tenet of all spiritual practice is the induction of calming states. Prayer is often referenced as a way to center oneself, gain composure, and aid healing. Herbert Benson, however, was the first to formally consider the use of meditative practices to enhance physical health. While at Harvard in the 1970s, Benson selected specific elements of Buddhist meditation and measured their efficacy at reducing stress. Through several well-designed studies, Benson discovered that meditative practices, such as deep breathing, repetition, and progressive muscle relaxation, do indeed reduce stress. Benson's work has been extended to what we now know as the "relaxation response" and has been successfully used to treat hypertension, panic, cardiac arrhythmias, anxiety, depression, pain, anger, and even PMS.

Benson, and many others, have further demonstrated that hypnosis, Zen practice, Transcendental Meditation, and progressive muscle relaxation all decrease oxygen consumption, respiratory rate, heart rate, and blood pressure.

Faith also appears to be linked to immunity and has long been pointed to as a complement to traditional treatment measures. In a 1988 clinical study of women undergoing breast biopsies, the women with the lowest stress hormone levels were those who used their faith and prayer to cope with stress.[15]

For this reason, the act of prayer has been utilized as a methodology to treat a host of illnesses. In a 1996 poll, one half of doctors reported that they believe prayer helps patients, and 67 percent reported praying for a patient.[16] Several studies have also looked at intercessory prayer (asking a higher power to intervene on behalf of another either known or unknown to the person praying, also called distance prayer or distance healing).[17] Although it is particularly difficult to study the effect of distance prayer, current research in coronary care units (intensive care units in hospitals devoted to people with severe heart disease, like those who have just suffered a heart attack) suggests that there is benefit. Compared to those who were not prayed for, patients who were prayed for showed general improvements in the course of their illness, less complications, and even fewer deaths.[18]

Another way in which spiritual practice may affect health is through the practice of forgiveness, which is a central component of many faiths. While it may take on different terminology in each faith, forgiveness is essentially a release of hostility and resentment from past hurts. In 1997, a Stanford University study found that college students trained to forgive someone who had hurt them were significantly less angry, more hopeful, and better able to deal with emotions than students not trained to forgive. Another survey of 1,400 adults found that willingness to forgive oneself and others, and the feeling that one is forgiven by God, led to beneficial health effects. Further research has suggested that emotions like anger and resentment cause stress hormones to accumulate in the blood, and that forgiveness reduces this buildup.[19] Whether spiritual practice is used to reduce stress, improve immunity, or decrease hostility, it appears to have a significant and tangible effect on health.

Faith Improves Relationships

Many spiritual elements appear to facilitate relationships. Actions such as forgiving others, expressing gratitude, performing kind acts, and behaving morally are all linked to prosocial skills. The ability to "walk in another's shoes" is also highly correlated with a sense of empathy, which is an integral component of relating to and understanding another. Meditation also appears to enhance parietal lobe activity, which regulates one's sense of self in relation to others. Recognition of the "other" position, and the ability to resonate with others' thoughts and feelings, improves the ability to relate to and understand others.

Newberg and Waldman cite several studies demonstrating the connection between meditation and improved function of the anterior cingulate cortex, which acts as a mediator between thoughts and feelings. As they state, "Contemplative practices stimulate activity in the anterior cingulate, helping a person to become more sensitive to the feelings of others."[20]

Further research demonstrated that meditating on any form of love, including God's love, appeared to strengthen the same neurological circuits associated with compassion toward others.[21]

Better appreciating another's position, strengthening compassion, and increasing sensitivity to the emotions of others are all benefits that come through spiritual practice—and become palpably important in times of crisis.

Are Animals Spiritual?

In considering whether or not we are wired to be spiritual or if spirituality has any place in evolution, many have pondered the existence of what is known as a selfish gene. As the theory goes, if humans are inherently selfish, spiritual practices—especially those that include prosocial behaviors like forgiveness, altruism, and kindness—are not biologically adaptive and would have ceased to exist. As we know from previous chapters, this is not the case, as there is ample evidence that animals do engage in a variety of compassionate behaviors, that they appear to understand morality, and that they have a sense of fairness. We also know that reciprocal altruism and upstream reciprocity both appear to be favored over selfishness in interdependent social groups.

The question then becomes, do animals engage in spiritual practices beyond those that have direct social benefits, such as religious worship, prayer, or spiritual rituals?

Wondering about this question, famous primatologist Jane Goodall describes the waterfall dance of a chimpanzee in *The Encyclopedia of Religion and Nature* and wonders whether it is indicative of religious behavior, precursors of religious ritual. She describes a chimpanzee approaching one of these falls with slightly bristled hair, a sign of heightened arousal:

"As he gets closer, and the roar of the falling water gets louder, his pace quickens, his hair becomes fully erect, and upon reaching the stream he may perform a magnificent display close to the foot of the falls. Standing upright, he sways rhythmically from foot to foot, stamping in the shallow, rushing water, picking up and hurling great rocks. Sometimes he climbs up the slender vines that hang down from the trees high above and swings out into the spray of the falling water. This "waterfall dance" may last ten or fifteen minutes."[22]

Chimpanzees also dance at the onset of heavy rains and during violent gusts of wind. Goodall asks, "Is it not possible that these performances are stimulated by feelings akin to wonder and awe? After a waterfall display the performer may sit on a rock, his eyes following the falling water. What is it, this water?"[23]

Goodall's report is seconded by Delia J. Akeley, wife of the famous taxidermist Carl Akeley and author of *The Biography of an African Monkey* (1928), who writes:

"While the porters were busy cutting down the undergrowth to clear a site for the tents, I gathered an armful of flowers and maidenhair ferns. I was arranging them in a paraffin tin (my safari vase) when J. T., who was tied to the limb of a tree, attracted my attention by her excited manner and peculiar cries. In an effort to learn the cause of her agitation I climbed up beside her. To my dying day I shall not forget the remarkable sight that rewarded my climb. Scattered over the great roof, singly and in groups, were assembled hundreds of monkeys. With arms raised above their heads they sat like statues, facing the setting sun. Everyone in camp, even the porters who were hurrying to finish their task before dark, climbed into the trees to view the monkey assembly. We had not been watching long when an indescribable medley of sounds rose on the air and echoed through the forest. The animal world, led by a mighty monkey chorus, was voicing a hymn to the setting sun. Although I did not see chimpanzees among the distinguished gathering in the treetops, their piercing screams rose shrilly above the trumpeting of elephants and the babel of strange calls and cries that resounded on all sides. Almost as suddenly as the animal ritual began, it ended."[24]

And while spirituality requires feeling and thinking about a being, object, or presence other than the self, it would not be possible without a sense of other, which accompanies the development of empathy. Here again, we can look to numerous examples of animal behavior to witness accounts of feeling for another. In his classic book *Second Nature*, Jonathan Balcombe recounts the behavior of a young male chimpanzee:

"The early twentieth-century Russian psychologist Nadie Ladygina-Kohts raised a young male chimpanzee named Yoni. As is a young chimp's way, Yoni was often unruly, delighting in defying Nadie's authority. One of his favorite spots was the roof of her house, and Nadie's firm commands and entreaties to get him to come down were fruitless. Eventually, the psychologist discovered that the only way to get Yoni to come down was to appeal to the chimp's concern for her. By closing her eyes and pretending to weep, Yoni would leave his perch and hasten to Nadie's side to comfort her while looking around indignantly for the source of her upset. Appealing to Yoni's empathy turned out to be the only way to circumvent his defiant nature."[25]

Empathy also appears to be hardwired. Mirror neurons have been discovered in primates and cetaceans, which suggest that the same part of the animal's brain is stimulated when they perform an action as when they see another animal perform the same action. Swamp sparrows have also been found to possess mirror neurons, suggesting that the ability to sense and feel for another in the common ancestry of birds and mammals.[26]

Mice have also been shown to respond to witnessing the pain of another. When scientists injected irritant into the stomachs and paws of mice, other mice recognized and responded to their writhing responses and showed a heightened sensitivity to the same painful stimuli.[27, 28]

Spirituality Matters When Facing Setbacks

"If today you're in a funk...tomorrow you're much more likely to be spiritually inclined, to engage in spiritual practices and double down on your focus on things that transcend humanity."[29]

That's just the way setbacks affect us. When we can't see the way through, sometimes the only thing we can turn to is a belief, however irrational it may seem, that things will work out. But we may also find that our belief needs some reconsideration.

After all, we may have doubt. As one woman shared with me when faced with the collapse of her company and several years of feeling isolated and alone, "I just didn't feel like I had a reason to go on."

It's in situations like this that we come to realize most fundamentally how much we need spirituality. And making it through what seems impossible applies the principle of natural selection to faith. In short, we realize just which beliefs work and which ones don't.

We may ask broad questions that revolve around contexts of personal existence and transcendent dimensions—those that are much larger and more complex than ourselves. We may wonder why we are here and what is the purpose of our lives. We may ponder the nature of events, asking questions like "Do things always happen for a reason?" and "What is the reason?"

This transcendent feature of spirituality, and the questioning of meaning and life itself, is a hallmark feature of growth, one that is triggered by the seismic quality of the setbacks we face. As Kevin, whom we met in chapter 1, described, "There was a greater meaning in what happened to me than I could see at the time."

But setbacks also challenge something else about our faith. They very fundamentally disrupt our beliefs about behaving in a just and ethical manner. If we think, for example, that our pain is unjust, we may begin to question morality as a whole. In what trauma researcher Kent Drescher describes as a "moral injury," setbacks that cause suffering—especially those that seem inhumane, cruel, and violent—have the capacity to jeopardize our motivation toward kind behavior.[30]

But this is also why setbacks matter. Because they cause us to reconfirm our faith, to reconsider just why we should behave well and what behaving well means. As Sara, whom we met in chapter 1, stated, "I wanted to be really angry, and even felt like acting cruel, because what my husband did, I thought, was unfair. But I also had to come to terms with what type of person I really wanted to be."

Examining our beliefs about the self, others, and the world often leads to what Drescher calls "moral uncertainty," in which we are unsure of what moral principles or values now apply.[31] But this is also because setbacks affect us in a very fundamental way. It is the feeling that the rug is pulled out from underneath us, and we are confronted with beliefs, values, and principles that no longer apply. *We question what we used to believe. And we ask what we will believe now.*

Yet setbacks also make us question whether or not we can make it through and if we can ever return to a sense of normalcy. In recollections of their attempts to restore balance, many survivors report feeling unsure if they could make it. Certainly, in looking back at challenging events, many still have a sense of disbelief that they had overcome what happened, "not knowing how [they] did it."[32]

Disbelief about setbacks and the fact that we survived them naturally causes us to consider that there was something larger than ourselves that helped us make it through. This is well described in an account shared by Tedeschi and Calhoun:

"You think about getting through something like that and it's downright impossible to conceive of how you ever could. But that's the beauty of the thing. It's gonna have to be said because I believe that God got me through it. Five or six years ago, I didn't have these beliefs. And I don't know what I would do without Him now."[33]

With a deepened sense of spirituality and the feeling that there is something that transcends the self, we typically experience emotions that many describe as being distinct from other positive emotions in that they do not primarily concern the self, the self's goals, or normal petty concerns. These self-transcendent positive emotions also promote pro-social behavior and a desire to become a better person.

The ameliorative effect of self-transcendent emotions can also be seen through a deepened connection to something larger than the self that facilitates an increased sense of spirituality. Many studies suggest that certain specific positive emotions generate an upward spiral toward greater spirituality, which in turn leads to subsequent experiences of positive emotions. In this way, self-transcendent emotions and spirituality are different from what is typically believed about spirituality, in that the resulting positive emotions can lead to increased feelings of spirituality as opposed to feelings of spirituality causing more self-transcendent emotions.

And you don't necessarily have to believe in God—atheists can also experience growth; as described by Tedeschi and Calhoun, "We find greater engagement with the fundamental existential questions and engagement itself may be considered growth."[34] By pondering their beliefs about the self, others, and the world, those who go through difficult life experiences often have a richer and more complex moral history from which to draw from. As a result, they tend to become more morally developed themselves. In what Drescher describes as states of moral uncertainty, moral dilemma, and moral distress, a person is forced to confront the fundamental questions that Tedeschi and Calhoun note and find resolutions that will lead to a more highly developed sense of morality.

Whether experienced as a transcendent experience that deepens the sense of connection to something larger than the self, or a moral injury that leads to a more sophisticated sense of morality, spirituality is enhanced and refined through setbacks. Setbacks apply the survival pressure of life to spirituality, causing us to weed out the beliefs that do not sustain us through the deepest challenges and strengthen the ones that do. Ultimately what results is not just a clarification of what we believe, but a rich life experience that justifies our beliefs.

Eight

THE *LEVERAGE* RECAP

In this book, we've spent a lot of time covering the subject of setbacks, how they affect us, why we need them, and how we can learn to use them to our advantage. And we've pointed to a wide range of research and, hopefully, in the process, begun to look at setbacks differently and even consider some ways we can begin to use them to inspire growth. But we've also covered a lot of ground. So to help you recall the important points, this section includes a few different summaries of what we have covered.

Twitter Summary

Avoiding adversity is so outdated. *Leverage* teaches us to dive right into adversity to inspire appreciation, openness, strength, connection, and faith—the keys to growth.

Book Summary

Most people believe that it is best to overcome adversity, minimize failure, and quickly bounce back from setbacks. However, this belief only keeps us in fear of adversity and prevents us from utilizing our greatest asset—the ability to adapt. *Leverage* makes the case that the real secret to profound and dramatic growth lies in the *struggle of,* not the *victory over,* adversity. Battling with adversity develops the following skills:

1. Gratitude—to find joy and appreciation for life
2. Connection—to form deep and meaningful relationships
3. Personal strength—to recognize strengths as a combination of power and vulnerability
4. Openness—to see opportunities we had previously missed
5. Faith—a stronger connection with a purpose greater than ourselves

The *Leverage* Recap

Chapter-by-Chapter Summary

Chapter 1: What Are Setbacks and Why Do They Matter?
Setbacks have a profound and dramatic impact. They are remembered with greater intensity, are retained longer in our memory, elaborated with more details, and rehashed more frequently than positive events. But setbacks also do something else. Because they break down our fundamental beliefs—and in doing so, incite a critical reconsideration of fundamental beliefs, values, and goals—setbacks are the foreground of adaptation.

Chapter 2: The Shattered Vase Is the Fertile Ground
As children, we develop many assumptions about the world, and we go to great lengths to maintain them. Yet the assumptions we make, and the beliefs we live by, are prone to a host of what are known as cognitive biases—things that make us mispredict our happiness and make decisions based on an incorrect set of beliefs. Setbacks reveal our biases. And it is not until we know just where the faults in our logic lie that we can rebuild a set of beliefs that better serves us.

Chapter 3: When All Roads Are Blocked, We Must Carve Our Own Path
Setbacks make us face a lot of contradictions: Contradictions about the way things are supposed to work and the way they actually do, contradictions about what we believe should happen and what actually does happen, and contradictions about how we feel and how we act. But facing contradictions also faces us with another stark reality: that life is full of paradoxes. And it is in these paradoxes that we develop what is known as dialectical thinking, which also allows us to do many things, including to see things from multiple perspectives, to see that small changes lead to bigger changes, and to see that within ourselves there can be growth, even when we are struggling.

85

Chapter 4: The Gratitude Advantage

Unlike what we think, there is something about losing everything that uniquely puts life in perspective and profoundly raises gratitude. And when it comes to getting through some of life's toughest moments, gratitude comes with a host of advantages: it orients us to notice positives, it alters priorities, and it enhances purpose. And what we know from a host of animal studies is that reciprocal altruism and upstream reciprocity—the building blocks of gratitude—are built into our very nature. When it comes to facing adversity, gratitude offers considerable advantage—it increases forgiveness, enhances connection, and recalibrates priorities—all things that take the sting out of losses.

Chapter 5: Vulnerable Yet Stronger—The Paradox of Strength

We spend considerable amounts of time hiding, running from, and fearing vulnerability. Yet what setbacks do is face us—head on—with vulnerability. And unlike what we think of vulnerability, it has considerable advantages. Vulnerability allows us to learn, to be imperfect, and to take risks—all integral components of adapting to a set of changed circumstances. And vulnerability has a place in our evolutionary history: it is how we develop empathy. Empathy, and the ability to connect with others, is essential when it comes to facing setbacks.

Chapter 6: Connection—What We Crave the Most

We all seek connection, yet we avoid it in a multitude of ways. There are many reasons we are afraid: We may fear rejection, we may not trust others, and we may not trust ourselves. Yet when facing setbacks, we also come to realize how much we need people and how much we need to connect. And what connection offers evolutionarily—a neurological cascade that reduces stress, improves immunity, and enhances health—it also offers adaptively in the form of trust and restored intimacy, both vital when hit with adversity.

Chapter 7: Faith—Why It Matters

Many people will never confront the question of just what they believe about faith and why—until they have to. Here setbacks have a unique role: They make us explain just how we made it through something we didn't think we could. But they also make us answer the question of just why setbacks happen. Whether we answer that question in a religious or spiritual context, the result is the same—a deeper and clearer sense of faith. And faith has a place not just in our evolution but in the way we cope with adversity, because faith helps us transcend ourselves and connects us to something much larger.

Section Two

LEARN TO LEVERAGE

It's in our nature to adapt. After all, we've been doing it for years. One of the most fascinating things about evolutionary research, in fact, is just how expansive this ability is. We can look at the multitude of ways in which color, size, bone structure, head circumference, limb length, and physical ability have created an amazing array of variation—all of which responds to only one pressure. That is, the pressure to survive. With survival pressure comes a unique opportunity. And the opportunity is this: to master the ability to adapt to an unpredictable set of circumstances for the chance to stay alive. Inherent in this opportunity are all of the components that make staying alive possible. Because the changing landscape has all of the answers. Answers to questions such as What skills work now? What characteristics help in this situation?, and What strengths can be used to solve this problem? And should we pay attention, we will learn what our limitations are, what opportunities are now open to us, what we overlooked—perhaps missed in our assessment of the quality of our lives—the real measure of our strengths, who matters and why, and what matters and why. Every time things change, every time we are set back, we have a new piece of information, and we also have new skills to learn. And just as we are never finished being the fittest, we are also never finished learning and adapting.

This section of the book offers the *how* of adapting. It's how we take adversity and learn to leverage it—to develop skills that move us forward, that move us in the direction of survival. Sure, we could spend a lot of time learning how to avoid setbacks. But we could also deny that evolution happened, that life is static or responds to a set of predictable pressures. We should know at this point that evolution, life, and success do not follow a pattern. That is to say, we cannot possibly learn to predict setbacks. Nor can we learn to control or avoid them. Nor should we. While at times navigating still waters may seem illusively attractive, we wouldn't learn much. But more importantly, we'd be terribly unprepared should things change. Instead, we should turn to the skills that make change survivable and even strengthening.

But we should also change the way we look at setbacks. We should move beyond simply accepting them or learning to tolerate them. Setbacks, on the other hand, should be looked at as symbols. Setbacks should remind us that growth, like life, is not black and white. There is no denying that setbacks hurt, and the premise of this book is in no way to glamorize adversity or paint a picture that it is rosier than it really is. Certainly, people who go through setbacks do not portray them as desirable, and we should not go in search of them either. But those who have been through challenging—even devastating—losses do say this: *What we learn is a gift.* And we only learn it through being set back. What setbacks do offer is the experience of paradoxes and the growth that depends on them. When we own the bad and the good in difficulty, therein we see that progress does not follow a straight or predictable path. Being set back, we may reformulate our approach and continue in the same direction—with more information and enhanced skills. Or we may stop going in the same direction altogether and turn toward a different path—one that was not before considered. In either case, there will be difficulty—we will feel uncertain, fearful, doubtful, frustrated. We may become resentful, hateful even. And yet, there will be growth. We may come to realize strengths we hadn't before, limitations we had denied, opportunities we had missed. Our priorities may shift, aligning more closely to our goals. Our relationships will change, taking on a deeper meaning. And our sense of purpose may become clearer.

And we should also change what we do with setbacks. When they happen, we should not try to immediately overcome them. Nor should we glamorize winning the battle. Winning is fine, and so is overcoming adversity. But these things are not end products. They are not the outcome. Instead, they are part of the process. They are part of survival. And survival is not ever finished. Even more importantly, overcoming setbacks is never finished. Life, as we know, doesn't follow a predictable pattern, and therefore the skill we learn today could be of no use tomorrow. But what will be of use is the ability to adapt. And adaptation, like overcoming adversity, may take time. As it should. When it does, critical reconsideration can happen. We are given time to take stock of what didn't work, disregard information that doesn't apply, and make changes with a full array of information. The skills of learning are developed—how to tolerate uncertainty, how to take risks, how to be imperfect, and how to survive failure. And strengths have time to emerge—how to master the footwork, hone the pitch, and master the game. But most importantly, we should respond to setbacks as the sparks that ignite the flame of life.

We will now take a look at the skills of adapting.

Do Some Serious Reconsideration

When setbacks knock us sideways, we come face to face with a harsh reality: *something about what we're doing no longer works.* Perhaps we started with a set of beliefs that we thought would lead to happiness—only to find out that they didn't. Or maybe the case is more severe, and something entirely unpredicted happened. Setbacks, as we know, can be both chronic, taking a long time to build, or sudden—those that come with no warning. In either case, we are temporarily stopped in our tracks. And while we may not have been able to predict the events that transpired, or even have any power to change them, what we do know is this: *setbacks require some different thinking.* They require us to change our approach to fit the circumstances we are now up against. To begin, we are going to have to ask some pretty serious questions. Consider the following:

- What things did I used to believe that are no longer true?
- What things did I think would or should happen that did not?
- What have I been doing that I can do no longer?
- Have any of my abilities been obliterated?
- What was absolutely essential then, and what is absolutely essential now?
- Has the way I look at relationships changed? If so, how?
- Is there anything that matters less now? Is there anything that matters more now?

How you decide to reformulate your beliefs is completely up to you. The most important thing is that you recognize that some beliefs no longer serve you and reconsider what you might believe instead.

Take a Values Assessment

Setbacks often fracture not just our beliefs but our values. We can feel as if the very values that used to guide and define our life no longer apply. For example, if you used to value making money and pursuing advances in your career to the detriment of your marriage, and your partner leaves you, you might feel as though achieving wealth as a value is no longer so important. On the other hand, you may also feel as though trust and connection is now more important. So let's do what I call a values assessment. Begin by making a list of all of the values you can think of. Consider every area of your life, such as family, career, friendships, spirituality (or lack thereof), personal goals, hobbies, things you are passionate about, and so on. You can list anything from honesty and integrity to connection and trust. You can also list things such as acclaim, success, and feeling significant and appreciated. Once you have created your list, ask yourself the following questions:

- What values no longer seem important?
- What values now seem more important?

Once you have answered these questions, it's up to you how you proceed. The most important thing is that you now have a clearer sense of what you value.

Do a Priorities Ranking

Like values, priorities are often disrupted by setbacks. Sometimes this happens in subtle ways, such as learning that a project we were creating at work is no longer possible, and our focus shifts to other tasks of the job. And other times the shift is abrupt and jarring—such as losing a loved one unexpectedly, being fired without warning, or having a bad accident. In any case, setbacks make things that didn't used to be important now strikingly important. Consider the case of an equine veterinarian who broke her jaw in a cycling accident and can now no longer practice. Before, her most important priority might have been building her practice, and now what takes precedence is rebuilding her health.

So let's take a look at your priorities with what I call a priorities ranking. Start by listing the most important thing in your life, and put a number one next to it. Then write down the second most important thing and put a number two next to it. Continue with this list until you have listed ten items. Now step back and ask the following questions:

- Have any priorities become more important?
- Have any priorities become less important?

Once you have the answers, recreate the list, ranking the priorities as they now apply. Here again, where you go from here is up to you. What is important is that you have a clear idea of what your priorities are.

Do an Uncertainty Brainstorm

The tendency to tolerate uncertainty is universal to everyone. Yet some cultures, as a whole, tolerate uncertainty better than others. This tendency was first noticed by Geert Hofstede, author of *Cultures and Organizations: Software of the Mind.* Hofstede uncovered that some cultures prepare us to feel more comfortable with uncertainty than others. According to Hofstede, there are several factors that determine whether or not a culture has a high uncertainty avoidance. For example, cultures with a high uncertainty avoidance tend to have more laws and regulations than those with a low uncertainty avoidance. Additionally, cultures with high uncertainty avoidance tend to have more oppressed members, and members display less interest or participation in politics than those with a low uncertainty avoidance. Whereas cultures with a high uncertainty avoidance tend toward very strict and specific laws and rules, those with low uncertainty avoidance have more political interest from members, as participation, and even protest, is seen as a vehicle for change.[1]

In education, cultures that rely heavily on educators to have the answers display high uncertainty avoidance compared to those where children are encouraged to be open-minded. High uncertainty avoidance in family life leads to role rigidity and well-defined patriarchal and maternal figures, while low uncertainty avoidance allows for greater flexibility in family and gender roles.

On an individual level, people with a high uncertainty avoidance often like clear and predictable rules, tend to be formal in interactions, have a strict and rigid schedule, and are resistant to change. These people prefer a careful, circumspect approach, do not like unpredictability, and tend to be more emotional. Conversely, people with low uncertainty avoidance abide by fewer rules, do not have a set routine or structure, are more informal in their approach, and are more open to change. These people feel much more comfortable with fewer rules, a more changeable structure, and often appear more calm and collected.

At this point, we should know that setbacks bring with them uncertainty. Familiar beliefs, values, and priorities often change in drastic and unexpected ways. In order to learn to adapt, you are going to have to build your tolerance for uncertainty. To do this, we are going to start by assessing your uncertainty avoidance. Respond to the following statements, giving yourself a rating from zero to ten, with zero meaning "not very much like me" and ten meaning "very much like me":

- I prefer having the answers.
- I prefer a set structure.
- I tend to take a planned approach to life.
- I prefer formality in interactions.
- I tend to avoid change.
- I avoid unusual or unknown situations.
- I prefer an orthodox approach as opposed to an unorthodox one.
- I prefer set roles.

Now tabulate your answers. While your score can be anywhere between zero and eighty, those with a score of forty or less tend to be low in uncertainty avoidance, while a score of forty or more can be described as high uncertainty avoidance. Ideally, in order to learn how to adapt, your score should be over forty, perhaps closer to sixty or seventy. Certainly, there is no set perfect score. However, very low scores do not permit change. And adapting to the changing circumstances setbacks bring requires that you be willing to try something different—and more importantly, something unproven. To do this, we are going to have to deal with uncertainty. So how do we build uncertainty? Let's try what I call an uncertainty brainstorm. To do this, first answer this question:

What one thing did the setback take away?

Your answer can be anything from a marriage, a child, a career, wealth, health, or a personal goal. Whatever the answer is, write it down. Now answer the following question:

What would you have done if you didn't lose_____?
(Write the answer from the first question here.)

Answer this question, listing as many possible options as come to your mind. For example, if your question was, *what would you have done if you didn't get married?* your answer could be anything from travel, go to school, start a business, or pursue a life passion. On the other hand, if your question was, What would you have done if you didn't become wealthy? your answer might be volunteer, join the peace corps, live more simply, or live in a different location altogether. The goal is to list as many different options as you can think of. Once you have written each option down, move on to the next part of the exercise.

Starting with the first option, consider each one as completely as possible. Take each one separately and visualize what it would be like to start a business, travel, volunteer, live off the land, and so on. As you do this, write down your reactions to each option, beginning with your initial thoughts and adding any thoughts that follow. For example, your initial reaction to traveling may be that it would be costly, but as you think it over, you start to feel excited about it and perhaps even look forward to exploring where you might travel. Whatever your reactions are, write them down. Then go back and look over what you wrote down. Do your answers reflect a resistance to change? Do you tend to focus on what is wrong with each option? Or perhaps why things won't work? If so, reconsider each of your options, and ask the following questions for each one:

- What could be one benefit of doing this?
- What could be one thing I learn from doing this?
- What is one positive thing that could happen unexpectedly?
- Is there something I could see myself enjoying about this?

The goal of these questions is to begin to shift your attitude toward uncertainty. When you can see that each option could have a hidden benefit, allow you to learn something new, or offer hidden enjoyment, you can also start to view uncertainty as something that leads to new discoveries—the discovery of valuable information about yourself, what makes you happy, and what will lead to the life you want. And more importantly, you can start to see uncertainty as an important part of adapting.

Do a Setback Storyline

Dialectical thinking begins with the idea that life is full of contradictions. The premise is that nothing is ever just one way. No situations, therefore, can be called "all bad" or "all good." Instead, every situation consists of both positive and negative characteristics. In fact, according to strict Fichtean dialectics (remember from chapter 3), the very existence of any one thing depends on the presence of opposite forces. Without light, there would be no darkness. And without darkness, there would be no light. The reason is that in order to understand anything, and qualify its characteristics, we have to have something to compare it to. For example, if there is only light, and no darkness, then it is impossible to call something lighter than anything else, because everything is light. Yet dialectical thinking is not natural to us—especially when faced with adversity. In many ways, we are oriented to classify things as "either/or" simply because it makes understanding them much easier. Laws, for example, are very hard to interpret as being "partly wrong and partly right." Rules in any group setting also tend to be inflexible and not open to interpretation, because order depends on them. And on an emotional level, setbacks hurt, and pain, as we know, has a profound way of encouraging us to focus on it.

But we should also know by now that looking at setbacks as all bad does not help us cope with them—and in many ways, it impedes adaptation. In order to be willing to try new approaches, which is a crucial part of adapting, you are going to have to see setbacks from multiple perspectives. This doesn't necessarily mean that you have to "find the good" in what often feels like bad news. But it does mean that you are going to have to see the opportunity—sometimes more than one—hidden in every setback. To do this, we are going to do what I call a setback storyline.

Begin by writing down the events of your setback in one sentence. For example, you can say, "Man fell in love, got married, had two children, and his wife left him." Or you can say, "Woman lived her whole life wanting to be a gymnast, only to break her leg in practice." Try to be as concise as possible, incorporating all relevant details into one summarizing sentence. Once you have your sentence, you are going to add one more. In this next sentence, you are going to complete the story any way you like. For example, if your first sentence is "Man fell in love, got married, had two children, and his wife left him," your second sentence could read, "Man went traveling with a friend, fell in love with hiking, and started an adventure company." You are going to do this five times until you have five different stories.

When you are done, you should have five alternative perspectives on the same setback. Again, what you write, and how you complete the story, is up to you. There are no right or wrong answers. If you find you get stuck, you can also ask a trusted friend to help come up with story completions. The goal is to be able to look at the situation in many different ways, from multiple perspectives. What you will find is not just that a story can be told in many different ways, but that any situation, even a very challenging or heartbreaking one, can be considered from multiple perspectives. When it is, it can also be completed it many different ways. And focusing on how you complete the story—as opposed to the frustrating setback itself—orients you toward the beliefs you need to reconsider, the skills you need to learn, and the actions you need to take—all essential skills of adapting.

Take a Mental Detour

Recall that we learned in chapter 2 that failure to make peace with our losses often leads to a tendency to take wild and unmeasured risks. However, even when we do recognize a setback for what it is, trying something new is often not our first response. Rather, many of us simply do more of the same. We redouble our efforts, put in more time, and invest more energy. The tendency to avoid changing strategy can be partly accounted for by what behavioral economists call "sunk costs." Sunk costs account for all of the time, energy, and money we have *already* devoted to the task. Perhaps we have spent several years trying to start a business. Maybe we have invested several years of schooling and have considerable student loan debt only to be faced with the harsh reality that we cannot secure a job in our field. Situations like this play to the natural tendency to "get out what we have put in." Which means staying the course. We may also exhibit "loss aversion," which is the desire to avoid any further losses. Once we know we have already suffered a significant loss, we hesitate to try anything new—for fear of losing more than we already have. Yet adapting, as we know, depends on being willing to alter the strategy without any guarantee of success. In short, we are going to have to be willing to take a measured risk, or several, until we find what works.

But we are also going to have to be open to new experiences, because they offer the chance to discover something that we didn't realize we enjoyed. To do this, we are going to do what I call taking a mental detour.

You are going to begin by recalling five happy memories from your childhood. These can be anything from family vacations, summer pastimes, hobbies, playing sports, or time with friends. Next, I want you to elaborate the memories with as much detail as you can remember. Write who was there, what you were doing, and where you were. Describe each component of the memory as completely as possible.

When you are finished, you should have five experiences that include some sort of activity, in a specific place, with or without others. For most people, these memories will usually involve some sort of shared experience that revolved around a mutually held goal. Common themes are things like organizing a party with friends, playing on sports teams, building something with others, or taking a class. However, there are no right or wrong answers. The goal is simply to recall five activities that you used to enjoy and that you found yourself immersed in.

Next, you are going to try each of these activities again. For example, if one of your memories is playing on a softball team as a kid, I want you to find an adult softball league and give it a try. Or if you recall enjoying building forts in the living room with a sibling or friend, I want you to build something again with somebody you enjoy spending time with. The experience may not match exactly what you described in your recollection; however, the general theme should be the same. Similarly, don't worry if you feel your skills are not what they used to be. The point is not to measure your success at remembering how to do things from your past; the goal is to become comfortable with trying new things, and perhaps to find something you enjoy doing again.

Setbacks, in many ways, are like roadblocks. And adapting depends on the ability to try something new, to be willing to take a detour—even through unfamiliar territory. Yet detours also offer the chance to see things differently, remember a road you might've traveled before, and perhaps rediscover something you love. Taking a mental detour, just like a physical one, encourages you to be open to changing course—to navigate around the roadblock (in whatever form it takes)—for the chance of finding something better.

Take the Volunteer Test

Setbacks can degrade our sense of confidence, invade our minds with doubt, suspicion, and worry, and make us feel as though we have very little left. We can feel as though we should have known better, seen it coming, somehow been better prepared, or avoided the whole thing altogether. Setbacks, as we know from chapter 1, can cause us to replay events, rehash memories, and devote more time and energy to them. All of this can make it very difficult to move forward. Yet, what we often fail to remember is that setbacks, like evolutionary extinction patterns, do not follow a pattern. Instead, as you may recall from chapter 2, they follow the "planning is impossible" model. Surely this doesn't mean that we should give up trying to prevent them or that we should not try to minimize losses when they do happen. But what it does mean is that we should understand that setbacks, inherently, do not come with warning signs. And, therefore, if we could have prevented them, we would have.

Adapting to setbacks, on the other hand, involves a "forward-focused" model that asks "Where do we go from here?" and avoids asking "Why didn't we know better?" In order to uncover where we go from here, we are going to have to get better at trying things we may not have tried before. To do this, we are going to *take the volunteer test.*

Consider the following question:

If money were not a factor, and I could volunteer my time anywhere I chose, what would I do?

Next, write down the first three things that come to your mind. You can list things like "help at the animal shelter," "volunteer at an elementary school," or "help at a homeless shelter." There are no right or wrong answers. The goal is simply to consider what you enjoy doing, regardless of the extrinsic payment attached to it. It is what you do just because you feel good doing it, not for any other reason. Answers to this question are typically autotelic in nature, meaning that they are rewarding in and of themselves. For this reason, autotelic activities do not require external motivating factors such as fame, power, or wealth. For example, you may enjoy rescuing dogs because it feels rewarding to you. Similarly, you may find yourself helping out at your child's school because, again, it *feels* rewarding to you.

What autotelic activities—like things that do not offer external rewards—do is ease the natural resistance to trying something different. Because the rewards for volunteering are internal, and the service you offer free of charge, evaluation of progress is measured in terms of *how you feel.* You answer questions like "Do I enjoy doing this?" "Do I feel good when I do it?" External evaluations, like money and status, become secondary.

Get Grateful

Setbacks, as we learned from chapter 2, can make us feel as if our beliefs have been violated. For this reason, when bad things happen, we can often feel as if we have been unjustly treated, singled out, or in some way dealt an unfair blow. And while setbacks are arguably unfair, not surprisingly, feeling that they are unfair derails adapting to them. What we should also know by now is that as long as we maintain the cognitive bias that setbacks should not happen, we will also collect evidence as to why they shouldn't happen to us. We may replay the negative events, fixate on them, ruminate over them—all to the tune of staying focused on them.

Adapting to setbacks, on the other hand, looks to the here and now, finds evidence for what was spared, and asks, "What we can we be grateful for?" In order to get better at finding things to be grateful for, we are going to use what Shawn Achor, Harvard professor and author of *The Happiness Advantage: The Seven Principles of Positive Psychology that Fuel Success and Performance at Work*, calls a gratitude list. According to Achor, when you keep a gratitude list, your brain begins to scan your environment for positive things, and it pays less attention to negative events.[2]

To do a gratitude list, you are going to write down three new things you are grateful for every day for twenty-one days. You can list things like your child's smile, your health, nice weather, a compliment someone gave you, your ability to help someone in need, or even simple things like a roof over your head and food on the table. There are no right or wrong answers. What is important is simply that you list three new things every day, and avoid repeating your answers.

Over time, what you will find is not just a greater variety of things to be grateful for, but finding them becomes easier. You become what Achor calls "more primed to the positive," and your brain simply gets better at getting grateful. And gratitude, as we know, is a powerful antidote in the face of setbacks.

Do a Vulnerability Strength Builder

Vulnerability, like many parts of adapting, requires us to take a risk. We have to venture into emotional uncertainty and face the fear that we could be rejected, hurt, shamed, or even abandoned. And we face our own defenses—all of the natural defenses we arm ourselves with to avoid vulnerability. And the tendency to run from vulnerability is never stronger than after a setback.

Yet while avoiding vulnerability is attractive when we seek to minimize our losses, safeguard our images, and avoid shame, the problem is, none of this helps us move forward. Instead, adapting to setbacks and owning our strength requires us to also own its counterpart, which is vulnerability. Owning vulnerability matters when we want to build strength, because vulnerability, as we learned in chapter 5, is crucial to learning how to adapt. Learning how to be vulnerable, however, can be a challenge.

To do this, we are going to do what I call a vulnerability strength builder. You are going to begin by making a few lists. Your first list will be titled "Physical Risks." Here you will write down all of the things that feel physically risky to you, listing items from least risky to most risky. You can write down things like "walk a mile" to "run a marathon," or "play one set of tennis" to "enter a tennis competition." List as many things as you'd like, making your list as extensive as you wish.

Now make a second list labeled "Emotional Risks," and again, list as many emotionally risky things that come to mind. You might write things like "sharing something I've never told anyone before" or "telling someone how I really feel." You can also list things like "asking someone for help" or "letting someone see me cry." Here again, place the actions that seem least risky at the top of your list and continue listing things with increasing risk as you proceed.

The last list you will make is called "Mental Risks"; these are things that require cognitive vulnerability and carry intellectual risk. Often listed here are things like "take an unfamiliar class," "learn a new language," or "find a solution to a novel problem." This list, like the other two, will be ranked from least risky to most risky.

You should now have three separate lists, each with several items. Next you are going to choose one risk from each list to complete over the course of the week. Each week, you are going to choose three more risks to take. You can begin with any risk you'd like; however, most people prefer to start small and work their way down. As you do, keep a few things in mind:

- Facing vulnerability requires courage. While this may feel like an exercise in vulnerability, it is actually an exercise in courage.
- The goal is to get better at being vulnerable and not necessarily to please people or make sure you get the response you want.
- Vulnerability is about being imperfect.

Getting better at getting vulnerable comes with a multitude of benefits. Taking risks, trying new things, and allowing imperfections are the skills of learning. But the willingness to let ourselves be seen also fosters connection, empathy, and understanding. And all of these things comprise the definition of courage—and adapting. And as you will remember from chapter 5, *the more completely we are challenged, the greater the opportunity we have for growth.*

Do a Relationship Litmus Test

For most people, feeling connected to those around us matters deeply. Yet, as we know from chapter 6, setbacks have a unique way of making us run from connection. Some associate the vulnerability adversity brings with weakness, sidestep disclosure, and use avoidance to cope. Others have been primed from early on to not just avoid vulnerability but to avoid having needs altogether. Still others associate the vulnerability connection requires—especially after a setback—with relinquishing control.

We should know by now that setbacks do two things when it comes to connection: They make connection vital, and they make it extremely challenging. In many ways, it is the ultimate paradox—we need others more now than ever, yet we are also incredibly afraid.

Adversity will test everything about connection: whether or not we feel heard, accepted, and understood, and certainly how much we can trust. As we know, some relationships will not weather the storm. Yet adapting is about finding out just who will stand by us and letting go of those who won't. In order to find out, we are going to do what I call a relationship litmus test.

To do this, you are going to list all of the people you know on one list, and on a second list, write down every person that you would feel comfortable disclosing about your setbacks to. You may find that while your first list is quite long, the second one is pretty short. Not surprisingly, most people have a large valance of relationships with only a few people they feel very connected to.

Once you have your two lists written, you are going to select the person from your second list that you feel most comfortable with and ask that person to meet with you. Do not explain why you are asking to meet, and make sure you schedule at least one hour of time. In the meeting, disclose as much as you are comfortable with about the details of what you are going through, how you feel, and what it is like for you to talk about it. Pay careful attention to how you feel as well as your friend's reaction. After you finish, ask yourself a few questions: Did you feel heard? Did you feel accepted? Did you feel as if your friend made an attempt to understand you? Did you feel judged in any way? Did you feel that you could ask for help if you needed to? Keep in mind that what is most important is how you felt in the interaction—that is, your perception. Also remember that there is no right or wrong way to feel. You are going to work your way down your second list, repeating the steps above with each person until you have identified the people you feel most connected to and most safe with.

As you go through this exercise, it's helpful to keep a few things in mind:

- Disclosing emotionally charged information is an exercise in trust, vulnerability, and connection.
- Not all relationships will survive adversity, and that is OK. Some people are more able to sit with difficult circumstances, charged emotions, and vulnerability than others.
- Not all people will be able to understand your reality. You will find some people can relate to how you feel better than others.
- You only need a few. The benefits that come from feeling heard, understood, and connected don't come from disclosing to

everyone. It only takes a select few who can truly be there to help you through.

While setbacks may test our relationships, they also make us poignantly aware of just what connection offers: the ability to trust when trust seems impossible, to expose ourselves in ways that terrify us, and to reach out and ask for help when others turn away. Yet the risks we have to take, the uncertainty we have to tolerate, and the willingness to continue despite failure are not just the skills of connecting; they are indelible skills of adapting.

Write a Sermon

We should know by now that there is not one clear definition of spirituality. Some people equate spirituality with a sense of a higher power, while others consider it linked to a set of moral principles that clarify behavior. Similarly, some people remain close to the religious beliefs they were raised with, while others question these beliefs or take up different ones altogether. Still others may not cling to any one belief, faith, or spiritual principle and instead prefer to hover in a state of questioning.

Yet we will also recall from chapter 7 that nothing tests our beliefs quite like setbacks do. For those who have a clear sense of faith, this might mean revisiting beliefs and reaffirming actions as well as a reliance on their beliefs to get through. When faith is not so well defined, setbacks can make us question what we do believe, and in searching for answers to those questions, come to a clearer sense of what spirituality means to us. In either case, we will have some spiritual reconsideration to do.

To help with this, we are going to do an exercise I call writing a sermon. Writing a sermon, just like it sounds, means preparing a three- to five-minute speech that incorporates your most deeply held beliefs. You can write this in any style you'd like, using biblical examples, real-life stories, anecdotes, or examples from your own life. Try to capture what you believe is most important to a purposeful and joyous life. Keep in mind that there is no right or wrong in spirituality. What is important, as in any sermon, is that your beliefs are expressed clearly and in a way that makes sense to you. Who your hypothetical audience will be is also up to you, and your sermon should not be written to appeal to any particular faith beyond your own. For example, if you were raised in a Catholic household, yet you find your spirituality defined somewhere between Catholicism and Buddhism, write the sermon that clarifies your beliefs as opposed to those you were raised with. Remember, this is an exercise for you to become clearer about your spirituality, and what you write should reflect that.

Once you have your sermon prepared, read it out loud a few times to yourself (certainly you can also read it to a trusted friend), listening to how it sounds and paying attention to how you feel speaking it. If it doesn't sound or feel right, revise it until it does. When you finish, your sermon should be something that you feel good saying—something that you feel you can truly believe in—as well as something that sounds right to you. Finally, it is important that your sermon have your voice, in that it comes from you.

Clarifying our beliefs, and knowing not just what we believe but why, becomes especially important after a setback. Adversity has a way of making us question not just our beliefs but ourselves. And adapting to setbacks requires us to ask some really tough questions about who we are, what matters to us, and, of course, what we believe. Being able to dive into these questions fully and take the time necessary—struggle with the uncertainty as long as it takes—to answer them is what adapting is all about.

Leverage Reading List: Twelve Essential Books

Adversity, as well as the struggle to better manage in the face of setbacks, is universal. While each of the books listed below offers a different take on failure, trauma, and the thirst for growth, each one also provides some powerful lessons when it comes to dealing with setbacks.

What Doesn't Kill Us: The New Psychology of Posttraumatic Growth
By Stephen Joseph
(Basic Books, 2013)

Interested in learning about how traumatic experiences can actually make us better? Stephen Joseph lays out not just the important research that supports posttraumatic growth but shows just what it looks like in real life. This book is an excellent resource for anyone interested in learning the fundamental concepts of posttraumatic growth. Here are the important takeaways:

- Traumatic experience leads to a qualitative shift in how we experience the world.
- Trauma can lead to a profound sense of gratitude.
- Losses can help us become more open to new experience.
- What challenges us emotionally also builds incredible strength.
- Trauma deepens the sense of connection we have with those around us.
- Spirituality is an integral part of coping with distress.

Supersurvivors: The Surprising Link between Suffering and Success
By David Feldman, PhD, and Lee Daniel Kravetz
(HarperWave, 2014)

What can we learn from those who seem almost impervious to whatever life throws at them? Feldman and Kravetz present a compelling argument for looking to the many processes these "supersurvivors" use to connect suffering and thriving. Along the way, we meet several people who have made extraordinary success out of great tragedy. What we learn is this:

- Positive thinking, when it overlooks reality, doesn't help.
- Perceiving that we are supported is just as important as having people around us.
- Supersurvivors use realistic expectations and "grounded hope" to thrive in the face of adversity.

The Rise: Creativity, the Gift of Failure, and the Search for Mastery
By Sarah Lewis
(Simon & Schuster, 2014)

Want to know just how "almost, but not quite" making it can help you? Through case studies and narrative discussion, Lewis very insightfully makes the case that failure is a gift on the path to success. A failure—or a "near miss," as Lewis calls it—offers a measure of our skills, revealing just where we have made improvements and where we still need to work. Lewis encourages us to look at several examples of near misses in everyday life—everything from "unplanned national parks" to the successes of many notable figures. When it comes to dealing with setbacks, Lewis offers some very important insights:

- We need near misses.
- Near misses are not misses, or failures, at all. Instead they are a necessary part of growth.
- Near misses often precede wins.

Broken Open: How Difficult Times Can Help Us Grow
By Elizabeth Lesser
(Random House, 2008)

It's tough to find a better argument for the connection between vulnerability and learning than Lesser's book. Lesser shows how when we are "opened up," we are also ready to hear, experience, and act in new ways. In terms of coping with trauma and adversity, here is what we can learn from Lesser:

- Trauma is in many ways a catalyst for powerful self-growth.
- Vulnerability is an important part of learning.
- Vulnerability helps us to learn to act in new ways.

One Life to Give: The Path to Finding Yourself through Helping Others
By Andrew Bienkowski
(The Experiment Press, 2010)

Just how does giving back affect us, and why do we need it? Bienkowski's book very eloquently shows that giving back adds a very important ingredient to a happy and meaningful life: gratitude. When it comes to facing adversity, Bienkowski provides some pretty important insights:

- Gratitude helps us feel connected to those around us.
- Giving of ourselves provides purpose and meaning.
- Helping others overcomes a host of negative feelings.

Flow: The Psychology of Optimal Experience
By Mihalyi Csikszentmihalyi
(Harper Perennial, 2008)

If you've ever wondered what's missing in your life, or why sometimes you struggle to stay present, the answer is probably flow. Csikszentmihalyi, who is well known for his groundbreaking work on optimal experience, helps us understand just what it means to be in "flow," and how, when we are there, we're exhilarated, alive, and, interestingly, protected from a host of illnesses, depression, and even addiction. When it comes to living a happy life, Csikszentmihalyi offers this:

- People who experience flow more often report being happier, less depressed and anxious, and are less likely to engage in addictive activities.

- Children who have higher levels of flow are better adjusted.
- Flow is a state that is defined by these conditions: a challenging activity that requires skill, the merging of action and awareness, clear goals and feedback, total concentration, a feeling of total control, a loss of self-consciousness, and the transformation of time.
- Even everyday tasks can be turned into flow-inducing activities.

Mindset: The New Psychology of Success
By Carol Dweck
(Ballantine Books, 2007)

There are two kinds of mind-sets a person can have—fixed or growth. According to Dweck, those with fixed mind-sets see ability as a set state and are unable to adapt in the face of challenge. Those with a growth mind-set, on the other hand, see adversity as an opportunity for growth and their ability as something that can be developed. Pointing to a massive amount of research, Dweck offers these insights:

- People with growth mind-sets view challenge as an opportunity.
- To create a growth mind-set, eliminate any negative voice that may be telling you that you cannot improve or overcome a setback.
- Having a growth mind-set means believing that you can improve with time and effort.

Open: An Autobiography
By Andrei Agassi
(Vintage, 2010)

Agassi's touching memoir takes us through his early years with his controlling father, the unending pressure to perform, and the frustration, depression, and even addiction that resulted. Then he shows us just how he took his life back. Beyond a brilliantly told and riveting story, Agassi makes some very powerful points:

- You are at your best when you play the game for yourself.
- Having to be perfect derails performance.
- Worrying about losing kills the joy of the game.
- No one can know what is best for you but you.

Learned Optimism: How to Change Your Mind and Your Life
By Martin Seligman
(Vintage, 2006)

Former president of the American Psychological Association, Seligman is well recognized for his pioneering work on positive psychology. If you have even the slightest interest in learning how to incorporate positive psychology in your life, this book is a must-read. Seligman deftly lays out how what we attribute failure and success to (what we say to ourselves about these things) affects not just how we feel but how likely we are to ultimately succeed. Seligman offers not just solid evidence—the amount of research he has compiled is outstanding—but also tools to assess your optimism level and to get better at getting optimistic. Here are the main points:

- What we say to ourselves about success and failure determines how we respond.
- Those who manage failure well do three things: They don't take it personally, they don't let it become pervasive, and they don't see it as permanent.
- Optimists respond to success in three ways: They attribute it to themselves, they see success as long lasting, and they allow success to boost other areas of their lives.

Wild: From Lost to Found on the Pacific Crest Trail
By Cheryl Strayed
(Vintage, 2013)

In this fascinating book, Strayed makes no attempt to disguise the pain of losing her mother, in many ways her best friend. Instead, she takes us right into the heart of uncertainty as she traverses the Pacific Crest Trail and shows us that not having the answers, and not even knowing where you are headed, can lead to some pretty profound insights. Here is what Strayed has to offer:

- There are no predictable reactions to devastating loss.
- Loss often makes us question everything about ourselves, our lives, and the world around us.
- Being uprooted, confused, and even lost, can all precede finding what really matters.

Man's Search for Meaning
By Victor Frankl
(Beacon Press, 2006)

There is perhaps no book that explores the ways in which searching for meaning in the aftermath of crisis is not just a spiritual crisis but a very human one. Drawing on his training as a psychiatrist, Frankl dives right into the heart of his story: his three years spent in concentration camps, including Auschwitz, and losing his parents, brother, and pregnant wife. Frankl shows us how he learned to find meaning in what could only be described as horrific circumstances, and how it was this—expressed in the desire to complete his manuscript—that ultimately compelled him to survive while others perished. While this book is much more than an incredible story, here are the main insights:

- The search for meaning is universal.
- When we can find meaning in suffering, it ceases to be suffering.

When Bad Things Happen to Good People
By Harold Kushner
(Anchor, 2004)

If you have ever asked, "Why do bad things happen?" Kushner's book is a must-read. In his gripping account of learning that his infant son has an incurable degenerative disease, Kushner faces all of the doubts, fears, and questions that surround tragedy. As he does, he offers clear-headed hope and solace to us all. Here is what we can learn:

- Not everything happens for a reason.
- We live in a world where things don't always make sense.
- Not everyone—relatively few in fact—are equipped to understand senseless acts.
- Aphorisms like "It's all in God's plan" evolved to keep an inherently disordered world in order.
- Instead of asking God why bad things happen, we should be asking him to help us.

Real-Life Examples: Ten People Who have Leveraged Adversity

While I have compiled a list of ten people who have taken extremely challenging situations and used them to inspire dramatic growth and, in the process, achieved truly amazing things, for every recognizable figure included here, there are many, many more.

Amy Purdy

At age nineteen, Amy Purdy was at the top of her snowboarding career. Then, without warning, she contracted bacterial meningitus, went into septic shock, and lost both of her legs below the knee, both kidneys, and her spleen. At that time, doctors gave Purdy a 2 percent chance of survival.

Yet Purdy did survive, and she was determined to return to the board. While the first few attempts were disastrous—at one point her prosthetic leg went tumbling down the mountain—Purdy persevered, and in one short year after losing her legs, she returned to major competition, finishing a remarkable third place. Soon, news of her amazing accomplishment traveled, and she received a grant from the Challenged Athletes Foundation (CAF), which enabled her to continue competing throughout the United States. Shortly thereafter, Purdy became a CAF spokesperson and advocate for amputees. Purdy later founded her own nonprofit organization, Adaptive Action Sports, to support other athletes, artists, and musicians with physical disabilities.

In 2011, Purdy gave a powerful TED talk called "Living Beyond Limits" detailing her story, and in 2014, she was named one of ESPNW's Impact 25. Later that year, Purdy secured a bronze medal in the 2014 Winter Paralympics in the snowboard cross event.

Purdy's full story can be read in her gripping memoir, *On My Own Two Feet: From Losing My Legs to Learning the Dance of Life,* released in 2014 by HarperCollins.

What We Can Learn

Setbacks lead to unrecognized opportunities. As Purdy says in her TED talk, before losing her legs, she used to think if she ever had to be in a wheelchair, she would "wheel myself off a cliff," yet now, looking back, she offers, she "wouldn't change a thing."

Bethany Hamilton

Before the age of thirteen, Hamilton was already a rising star. She had won two major surfing competitions and was well on her way to a competitive career. But at just thirteen, Hamilton's life also changed dramatically when a fourteen-foot tiger shark bit off her left arm. Although rushed to the hospital immediately, Hamilton still suffered massive blood loss and went into hypovolemic shock. While the hospital recovery took one week, amazingly, Hamilton was back on her surfboard just one month later. At first Hamilton used an adapted surfboard with a handle for her right arm and learned to kick more to make up for the loss of her left arm. In her first return to competition after losing her arm, Hamilton finished an amazing fifth and went on to rack up an incredible record, three times besting the field in major competition. In 2004 she won the ESPY Award for best comeback athlete and also received the Courage Teen Choice Award.

Hamilton's book, *Soul Surfer: A True Story of Faith, Family, and Fighting to Get Back on the Board,* was published in 2004 by MTV books, and the movie, *Soul Surfer,* documenting her amazing journey, followed shortly thereafter. Her story is also told in the 2007 documentary *Heart of a Soul Surfer,* directed by Becky Baumgartner.

What We Can Learn

Spirituality is a part of finding meaning in the aftermath of setbacks. While Hamilton had always been a spiritual person, after her attack, she recounts turning to her Christian faith to find meaning and to begin to recreate her life.

Jim Carrey

While many easily recognize Carrey as the hysterical star of many Hollywood blockbusters, few know that things were not always so easy for him. From the time he was very young, Carrey's family struggled to make ends meet, and when his father, an unemployed musician, could no longer support the family, Carrey had to drop out of school to help out. Eventually the family found themselves living in a van, yet even then, Carrey had a vision. In the beginning it was his dad driving him to comedy clubs in the Toronto area, but when his first act bombed, he questioned his ability. But Carrey worked on his craft and soon returned to the stage, polished and prepared. When Rodney Dangerfield noticed Carrey and signed him as an opening act for his tour, that's when his career got a needed boost. Carrey went on to perform at *The Comedy Store, An Evening at the Improv,* and *The Tonight Show.*

Yet when Carrey turned his focus toward acting, he hit roadblocks again. In his first audition for *Saturday Night Live,* he was passed over. Carrey did land roles in several low-budget films and a recurring role on the NBC sitcom *The Duck Factory,* which was canceled after just one season. Carrey persevered, however, eventually meeting Damon and Keenan Wayans and landing a recurring role in their sketch comedy, *In Living Color.* Carrey stuck it out for three years and was one of the few remaining actors when he finally got his first big break: a starring role in the major motion picture *Ace Ventura Pet Detective.*

What We Can Learn

Setbacks cause critical reconsideration. Carrey's first act didn't make it. And while he had a choice to give up, instead he chose to look at what didn't work, make the needed changes, and keep at it.

Oprah Winfrey

Considered by some to be the most influential woman in the world, Oprah was not handed anything. Born to a teenage mother and raised in poverty, Winfrey was also reportedly molested from the age of nine by an uncle, cousin, and family friend. When at age fourteen she became pregnant, she ran away from home. After her son died in infancy, Oprah moved in with the man she calls her father in Tennessee. After being transferred from the local high school to a more affluent one, Winfrey was subjected to teasing because of her obvious poverty. Yet after winning a teen beauty pageant and catching the eye of a producer, Winfrey was hired to coanchor the evening news—at just nineteen. During this time, Winfrey, who had graduated from high school with honors, won an oratory contest, which resulted in a full college scholarship. Soon recognized for her heartfelt and endearing delivery, Winfrey was moved to the daytime talk-show arena, where the then-third-rated Chicago talk show quickly rose to first place. Winfrey then launched her own production company, which became internationally syndicated. Winfrey has long been credited with being genuine and attuned to her audience and for having a more empathic approach to daytime television. For this reason, Oprah has often landed exclusive prime-time interviews that set viewing records.

What We Can Learn

Vulnerability is a strength. Oprah uses her vulnerability—she confessed the history of her molestations during a 1986 episode of her TV show discussing sexual abuse—to connect with her guests, who often find themselves revealing much more than they had previously. Winfrey's openhearted approach shows just how the courage to be vulnerable draws people in.

Jay Z

One of the most successful hip-hop artists in America, *Forbes* estimated Jay Z's net worth at $520 million. He has sold over one hundred million records and won more than nineteen Grammy awards. Yet Jay Z was raised in a housing project in Brooklyn, New York, he didn't graduate high school, and he has been shot at three times in his life. Although music was his love, and he had made appearances with Big L and Mic Geronimo, Jay Z couldn't get a deal of his own. No major record label would sign him.

So Jay Z created his own label, Roc-A-Fella Records, with Damon Dash and Kareem Biggs. When Jay Z released his 1996 debut *Reasonable Doubt,* it reached twenty-three on the Billboard 200, was named by *Rolling Stone* as one of the 500 Greatest Albums of All Time, and eventually hit platinum status. Since then, Jay Z has had multiple platinum albums and pioneered many successful businesses—he reportedly sold the rights to his clothing line, RocaWear, to Iconix Brand Group for $204 million. He also co-owns the 40/40 Sports Bar chain, is cobrand director for Budweiser, and is part owner of the Brooklyn Nets NBA team. Most recently, in 2013, Jay Z launched his own sports agency, Roc Nation Sports.

Now in retirement, Jay Z has turned his focus toward philanthropic pursuits, founding The Shawn Carter Foundation, which provides funding for those facing socioeconomic hardships to attend college. The rapper also reportedly donated one million dollars to the Red Cross after Hurricane Katrina.

As one of Jay Z's songs states, "the greatest form of giving is anonymous to anonymous." Jay Z's full story can be read in his 2010 memoir, *Decoded,* published by Speigel and Grau. Jay Z's story is also told by Zack O'Malley Greenberg in his book, *Empire State of Mind: How Jay Z Went from Street Corner to Corner Office,* released in 2011 by Penguin.

What We Can Learn

Success depends on adapting. While Jay Z's story is undoubtedly a rags-to-riches tale, and his presence in the hip-hop world nothing if not prolific, his best—if often unrecognized—acumen is his ability to see important industry trends, recognize what works and what doesn't, make modifications, and ultimately always stay one step ahead.

Steven Spielberg

While Spielberg has won three Academy Awards, been nominated for seven (in the category of best director), had nine films selected for a best picture Oscar, and been called one of the "100 Most Influential People of the Century" by *Time* magazine, few know that Spielberg had more than one major setback.

Beginning in high school, Spielberg was bullied, and because of his family's Orthodox Jewish faith, he was often the subject of antisemitic hatred. As Spielberg recounts, "In high school, I got smacked and kicked around. Two bloody noses. It was horrible." Later, when Spielberg twice applied to film school at University of Southern California School of Theatre, Film, and Television, he was rejected both times.

Instead, Spielberg chose to work as an unpaid intern—seven days a week—for Universal Studios, where he made his first short film, *Amblin,* which caught the attention of Universal Studios' vice president Sidney Sheinberg and resulted in Spielberg's first break: he became the youngest director to be signed to a long-term deal with a major Hollywood studio. However, Spielberg's first opportunity to direct a full-length film was halted when there was trouble casting the lead role, and ultimately the film was canceled. Finally, after his work on various television segments (such as *Columbo*) and made-for-TV movies (like *Duel, Something Evil,* and *Sugarland Express*) was noticed by studio producers Richard D. Zanuck and David Brown, they asked Spielberg to direct his first big hit, *Jaws.* Even then, the work on *Jaws* was nearly shut down due to delays and budget problems.

However, *Jaws* was an enormous success, winning three Academy Awards and grossing more than $470 million. It was then that Spielberg was in a position to choose his collaborative projects, and he later went on to amass one box-office hit after another, like *Close Encounters of the Third Kind, Star Wars, Raiders of the Lost Arc, Indiana Jones, E.T., Poltergiest, The Twilight Zone, The Goonies, Gremlins, The Color Purple, Batman, Jurassic Park*, and *Schindler's List*.

With his massive success, Spielberg turned to philanthropic efforts, such as the Shoah Foundation, which archives the testimony of Holocaust survivors, the Starlight Foundation, which uses technology-based entertainment and education to improve the lives of sick children, and a merit badge for cinematography program for the Boy Scouts of America.

Beyond his film recognition, Spielberg has also received several awards for his work, including the Federal Cross of Merit with Ribbon of the Federal Republic of Germany for his work on *Schindler's List,* an honorary degree from Brown University, the Department of Defense Medal for Distinguished Public Service, an honorary Knight Commander of the Order of British Empire by Queen Elizabeth II, a knight of Legion d'honneur by president Jacques Chirac, and he was admitted as a commander of the Belgian Order of the Crown.

And unsurprisingly, more than thirty years after his initial rejection from the University of Southern California Film School, he was awarded an honorary degree. It was then, in 2012, that Spielberg admitted that he had one more major handicap—he is dyslexic.

What We Can Learn

Setbacks can change our priorities. After applying to USC twice, and getting rejected both times, it was clear—something had to change. What might have been Spielberg's initial priority, getting into film school, now took a backseat to what then became important, which was getting as close to moviemaking as possible. Lucky for us, Spielberg choose to become an intern—forgoing pay—to follow his craft in his own way.

Shia LaBeouf

While many know LaBeouf as Sam Witwicky from the *Transformers* movie, LaBeouf's life has been anything but easy. While he describes his past now as a "good childhood," LaBeouf actually grew up facing poverty, emotional abuse, and drug addiction. At one point, after LaBeouf's parents divorced, and his mother was struggling to make ends meet, his uncle had planned to adopt him. LaBeouf's father, a Vietnam veteran, also fought a heroin addiction and reportedly had violent flashbacks—once holding a gun to his son's head.

Yet LaBeouf was crafty. Initially starting his comedy routine to bring laughter to a very stressed household, LaBeouf got the idea to become an actor after witnessing the success of an acting friend. Hoping to solve his parents' money troubles, LaBeouf found an agent in the yellow pages and landed representation after impersonating his own manager.

When LaBeouf was cast on the Disney Channel's weekly program *Even Stevens* and later won a Daytime Emmy Award, he gained recognition among teen audiences. However, when he landed the role in *Disturbia*, he soon became a household name. LaBeouf went on to star in several other hit movies, such as *Indiana Jones and The Kingdom of the Crystal Skull*, *Transformers,* and Oliver Stone's *Wall Street: Money Never Sleeps.*

What We Can Learn

Setbacks lead to important adaptation. For LaBeouf, it was the difficult environment in which he was raised that created the need to find an escape—through comedy. What LaBeouf ultimately found, however, was much more than an escape; it became a well-honed skill.

Ashley Judd

Judd is well known not just for her family's musical accomplishments (Naomi and Wynonna are both accomplished country-music singers) but for her leading roles in movies such as *Ruby in Paradise, Norma Jean and Marilyn, Where the Heart Is,* and *Divergent.*

But when Judd was born, her mother was actually unemployed. Her parents divorced when she was just four, and by the time she entered college, she had attended thirteen different schools. According to a recent review of Judd's memoir *All That Is Bitter and Sweet,* "She [Judd] was left alone so much with her mother and sister touring the country to make it. Something suffers, and it was Ashley's childhood."

Yet when Judd read the first three lines of *Ruby in Paradise,* she knew the role of Ruby Lee Gissing, a young woman trying to make a new life for herself, was meant for her. Although she had limited experience and recalls being so nervous on the way to the audition that she nearly crashed her car, Judd got the part and received rave reviews for her work. She was later cast in several popular movies, such as *Smoke, Heat, The Passion of Darkly Noon, Norma Jean and Marilyn, Someone Like You, High Crimes,* and *Divergent.*

Judd has also gone on to pursue humanitarian work. She is a global ambassador for YouthAIDS, on the leadership council for International Center for Research on Women, and has narrated three documentaries on the Discovery Channel on the subject of YouthAIDS. She has also been involved with Women for Women International and Equality Now.

What We Can Learn

Setbacks can ignite the desire for connection—to reach out, help others, and give back—all of which helps us heal. In her words, "I had no idea there was help for someone like me, without an identifiable addiction or dependency. It is thus very important to me to speak without shame and stigma about depression, codependency, and adult-child issues, because I have now been taught we are only as sick as our secrets. Because someone carried the message of recovery to me, and helped me begin to learn about family systems and how affected I was by other people's addictions of various kinds, I have learned that I, too, can recover! Who knew?! It is a wonderful, miraculous thing!"

Eminem

With over 155 million albums and singles sold worldwide, Eminem is the sixth-best overall selling artist in the United States and the best-selling hip-hop artist. He has had ten number-one albums on the Billboard 200 list, has been ranked eighty-third on *Rolling Stone*'s list of the top one hundred artists, and has been dubbed the "King of Hip-Hop."

And few have been as outspoken about their setbacks as Eminem. Born to a teenage mother, Eminem's young life was never stable: his parents played in a band, lived a transient life, and ultimately divorced. With no contact from his father (Eminem's letters came back "return to sender"), Debbie, his mother, struggled financially and moved from house to house, often staying less than a year in any one place. When Eminem and his mother finally settled in Warren, Michigan, he found himself in a lower-middle-class neighborhood that was mostly black. Described by family members as "a bit of a loner," Eminem was often bullied and, at one point, he was beaten so badly that he suffered a severe head injury. He struggled in school, too, eventually dropping out at age seventeen to get a job and help his mother pay bills. But things were unstable there, too, as he and his mother frequently fought, and she eventually kicked him out. After becoming close to an uncle, who later committed suicide, Eminem was so affected that he didn't speak for days and avoided the funeral.

But during this time, Eminem also developed an interest in hip-hop and began collaborating with a high-school friend, often attending freestyle rap battles and open-mic nights. Gaining the approval of an almost exclusively black underground scene, Eminem was recruited to join several groups and was eventually signed by FBT Productions, which released his first album, *Infinite*. Yet *Infinite* was no big success, and Eminem was told to "try rock and roll." During this time, he was also struggling to make ends meet, working for minimum wage to raise his newborn daughter, Hailie. Although reportedly a model employee, he was fired from his job five days before Christmas and forced to move back into his mother's mobile home, where he turned to drugs and alcohol, which eventually led to an unsuccessful suicide attempt.

Yet Eminem channeled his rage into his debut EP, *The Slim Shady EP*, released by Web Entertainment. While the album was powerful, it did not take off. Later that year, Eminem was evicted from his home, and, with few options, he traveled to Los Angeles to compete in the Rap Olympics. After Eminem won second place, a staff member at Interscope Records played *The Slim Shady EP* for Dr. Dre, renowned rap icon and founder of Aftermath Entertainment. Dr. Dre loved what he heard and collaborated with Eminem to produce his first big hit, *The Slim Shady LP*, which went triple platinum that year. Eminem's next album, *The Marshall Mathers LP* broke Snoop Dog's record as the fastest-selling hip-hop album and Britney Spears's record for fastest-selling solo album in United States' history. His next album, *The Eminem Show,* hit number one on the charts, sold more than 1.332 million copies in the first week alone, and was later certified ten times platinum by the Recording Industry Association of America. Eminem has had a total of seven albums that debuted at number one on the Billboard 200 chart with *The Marshall Mathers LP 2* reaching the second-largest debut sales week of the year, making Eminem the first lead artist since The Beatles to have four singles score in the top twenty of the Billboard Hot 100 chart. *The Marshall Mathers LP 2* later won best rap album at the fifty-seventh Grammy Awards.

Also an accomplished actor, Eminem played himself in *8 mile,* *Entourage* season-seven finale, "Lose Yourself," and *The Interview* with James Franco, and later founded a charity called the Marshall Mathers Foundation, which assists troubled youth.

Eminem's complete story can be read in his revealing memoir, *The Way I Am,* which was published in 2008 by Plume.

What We Can Learn

Adversity helps us embrace paradoxes. Eminem's creative process has long been fueled by the many setbacks he faced. While at times infuriating, and at others heartbreaking, Eminem never ceases to use his hardships to inspire profoundly powerful music.

Jennifer Hudson

She is a Grammy Award–winning singer with two certified gold albums and record sales exceeding one million copies worldwide. She has starred in several films, including *Dreamgirls, Sex in the City, The Secret Life of Bees,* and *Winnie Mandela,* collecting an Academy Award for best supporting actress, a Golden Globe Award, a Screen Actors Guild Award, and an NAACP Image Award.

Yet it was not always that way. While she had received considerable attention for her appearance on *American Idol,* she was rejected from the show. Adding insult to injury, Hudson also received criticism for her weight.

Hudson, however, was unfazed, and in 2006, she performed the song "Over It" live on Fox Chicago Morning News, announcing that the song would be released on her first album—even though she had not yet been signed to any record label. Only a few months later, she was signed to Arista Records, and in 2008, she released her hit debut album, *Jennifer Hudson,* for which she won a Grammy Award.

Yet tragically, in 2008, the same year she won her first Grammy, Hudson's mother, brother, and nephew were shot and killed by her estranged brother-in-law.

While initially shocked—she took three months off—Hudson returned to the public eye and immediately announced the Julian D. King Gift Foundation in her nephew's memory. According to the organization's website, the purpose of the foundation is to "provide stability, support, and positive experiences for children of all backgrounds."

In 2010, Hudson also became a spokesperson for WeightWatchers and in 2012 released a memoir, *I Got This: How I Changed My Ways and Lost What Weighed Me Down* (published by Penguin Publishing Group), which describes her weight loss of more than eighty pounds.

In 2014, she was selected as the favorite humanitarian at the People's Choice Awards.

What We Can Learn

Faith helps us move forward when times are tough. According to Hudson, her faith was what helped her to keep moving forward when her world was tragically shattered. In her words, "Definitely it's my faith in God and growing up—my mother, even though she's not here now, she trained us well."

Endnotes

Chapter 1

1. S. A. Christianson, "Emotional Stress and Eyewitness Memory: A Critical Review," *Psychological Bulletin* 112, no. 2 (1992), 284–309.

2. C. S. Carver, M. F. Scheier, and J. K. Weintraub, "Assessing Coping Strategies: A Theoretically Based Approach," *Journal of Personality and Social Psychology* 56 (1989), 267–83.

3. J. Bruder, "The Psychological Price of Entrepreneurship," *Inc. Magazine,* June 2014.

4. A. Tugend, "Praise Is Fleeting, but Brickbats We Recall," *New York Times,* March 23, 2012.

5. T. M. Amabile and S. J. Kramer, *The Progress Principle: Using Small Wins to Ignite Joy, Engagement, and Creativity at Work* (Boston: Harvard Business Review Press, 2011).

6. S. A. Christianson and E. Loftus, "Some Characteristics of People's Traumatic Memories," *Bulletin of the Psychonomic Society* 28 (1990), 195–98.

7. D. Nivedita, T. Kavita, and A. Zadgaonkar, "Effect on Systolic and Diastolic Duration Due to Emotional Setback," *International Journal of Information Technology Convergence and Services (IJITCS)* 2, no. 1 (February 2012).

8. S. B. Hamann, "Cognitive and Neural Mechanisms of Emotional Memory," *Trends in Cognitive Sciences* 5, no. 9 (2001), 394–400.

9. D. L. Schacter, *Searching for Memory* (New York: Basic Books, 1996).

10. M. M. Bradley et al., "Remembering Pictures: Pleasure and Arousal in Memory," *Journal of Experimental Psychology: Learning, Memory, & Cognition* 18, no. 2 (1992), 379–90.

11. K. S. LaBar and E. A. Phelps, "Arousal-Mediated Memory Consolidation: Role of the Medial Temporal Lobe in Humans," *Psychological Science* 9, no. 6 (1998), 490–93.

12. F. Craik and R. Lockhart, "Levels of Processing: A Framework for Memory Research," *Journal of Verbal Learning and Verbal Behavior* 11, no. 6 (1972), 671–84.

13. F. I. M. Craik and E. Tulving, "Depth of Processing and the Retention of Words in Episodic Memory," *Journal of Experimental Psychology General* 104, no. 3 (1975), 268–94.

14. A. D. Baddeley, "Implications of Neuropsychological Evidence for Theories of Normal Memory," *Philosophical Transactions at the Royal Society* 298, no. 1089 (1982), 59–72.

15. L. J. Kleinsmith and S. Kaplan, "Paired-Associate Learning as a Function of Arousal and Interpolated Interval," *Journal of Experimental Psychology* 65, no. 2 (1963), 190–93.

16. T. Harford, *Adapt: Why Success Always Starts with Failure* (London: Picador, 2012).

Chapter 2

1. R. F. Baumeister and B. J. Bushman, *Social Psychology and Human Nature: International Edition* (Belmont, USA: Wadsworth, 2010).

2. J. Sandler, *From Safety to Superego* (London: Guilford Press, 1988).

3. C. M. Parkes, *The Place of Attachment in Human Behaviour* (New York: Basic Books, 1982).

4. R. Janoff-Bulman, *Shattered Assumptions: Towards a New Psychology of Trauma* (New York: Free Press, 2010).

5. Ibid.

6. H. Bless, K. Fiedler, and F. Strack, *Social Cognition: How Individuals Construct Social Reality* (Hove and New York: Psychology Press, 2004).

7. A. Tversky and D. Kahneman, "Judgement under Uncertainty: Heuristics and Biases," *Sciences* 185, no. 4157 (1974), 1124–31.

8. A. Tversky and D. Kahneman, "Extensional versus Intuitive Reasoning: The Conjunction Fallacy in Probability Judgement," *Psychological Review* 90 (1983), 293–315.

9. M. G. Haselton, D. Nettle, and P. W. Andrews, "The evolution of Cognitive Bias," in *The Handbook of Evolutionary Psychology,* ed. D. M. Buss (Hoboken, NJ: John Wiley & Sons Inc., 2005), 724–46.

10. D. Kahneman and A. Tversky, "On the Reality of Cognitive Illusions," *Psychological Review* 103, no. 3 (1996), 582–91.

11. D. Kahneman and A. Tversky, "Subjective Probability: A Judgment of Representativeness," *Cognitive Psychology* 3, no. 3 (1972), 430–54.

12. J. Jermias, "Cognitive Dissonance and Resistance to Change: The Influence of Commitment Confirmation and Feedback on Judgement

Usefulness of Accounting Systems," *Accounting, Organizations and Society* 26 (2001), 141–60.

13. D. Ariely, *Predictably Irrational: The Hidden Forces that Shape Our Decisions* (New York: HarperCollins, 2008).

14. Ibid.

15. D. Gilbert, *Stumbling on Happiness* (New York: Knopf, 2006).

16. A. Tversky and D. Kahneman, "Judgement under Uncertainty: Heuristics and Biases," *Sciences* 185, no. 4157 (1974), 1124–31.

17. G. Gigerenzer, "Bounded and Rational," in *Contemporary Debates in Cognitive Science,* ed. R. J. Stainton (Oxford, UK: Blackwell 2006), 129.

18. G. Gigerenzer and D. G. Goldstein, "Reasoning the Fast and Frugal Way: Models of Bounded Rationality," *Psychological Review* 103 (1996), 650–69.

19. V. Hoorens, "Self-enhancement and Superiority Biases in Social Comparison," in *European Review of Social Psychology,* eds. W. Stroebe and Miles Hewstone (Hoboken, NJ: Wiley, 1993).

20. E. E. Jones and V. A. Harris, "The Attribution of Attitudes," *Journal of Experimental Social Psychology* 3 (1967), 1–24.

21. Z. Kunda, "The Case for Motivated Reasoning," *Psychological Bulletin* 108, no. 3 (1990), 480–98.

22. M. J. Mahoney, "Publication Prejudices: An Experimental Study of Confirmatory Bias in the Peer Review System," *Cognitive Therapy and Research,* 1, no. 2 (1977), 161–75.

23. D. L. Schacter, "The Seven Sins of Memory: Insights from Psychology and Cognitive Neuroscience," *American Psychologist* 54, no. 3 (1999), 182–203.

24. T. Harford, *Adapt: Why Success Always Starts with Failure* (New York: Farrar, Straus and Giroux, 2011).

25. Ibid.

26. S. Joseph, *What Doesn't Kill Us: The New Psychology of Posttraumatic Growth* (New York: Basic Books, 2011).

27. Lawrence G. Calhoun and Richard G. Tedeschi, eds., *The Handbook of Posttraumatic Growth: Research and Practice* (New York: Psychology Press, 2006).

Chapter 3

1. L. Howard, *Williams, Hegel, Heraclitus, and Marx's Dialectic* (New York: Harvester Wheatsheaf, 1989).

2. Barbara Cassin, ed., *Vocabulaire européen des philosophies*, trans. M. K. Jensen (Paris: Le Robert & Seuil, 2004), 306.

3. G. Vlastos and M. Burnyeat, eds., *Socratic Studies* (Cambridge: Cambridge University Press, 1994), chap. 1.

4. V. I. Lenin, *On the Question of Dialectics: A Collection* (Moscow: Progress Publishers, 1980), 7–9.

5. S. Denton, *Ancient European Philosophy: The History of Greek Philosophy Psychologically Treated* (St. Louis, MO: Sigma Publishing Co., 1903), 116–19.

6. F. H. von Eemeren, "Anyone Who Has a View: Theoretical Contributions to the Study of Argumentation," *Argumentation Library,* vol. 8 (Dordrecht: Kluwer Academic, 2003), 92.

7. A. Manzo et al., "Dialectical Thinking: A Generative Approach to Critical/Creative Thinking" (paper, 42nd Annual Meeting of the National Reading Conference, San Antonio, TX, December 2–5, 1992).

8. A. J. Ayer and J. O'Grady, *A Dictionary of Philosophical Quotations* (Oxford, UK: Blackwell Publishers, 1992), 484.

9. R. C. Pinto, "Argument, Inference and Dialectic: Collected Papers on Informal Logic," *Argumentation Library,* vol. 4 (Dordrecht: Kluwer Academic, 2001), 138–39.

10. J. Rowan, "Dialectical Thinking and Humanistic Psychology," *Practical Philosophy* (July 2000).

11. J. M. E. McTaggart, *A Commentary on Hegel's Logic* (New York: Russell & Russell, 1964), 11.

12. A. Manzo et al., "Dialectical Thinking: A Generative Approach to Critical/Creative Thinking" (paper, 42nd Annual Meeting of the National Reading Conference, San Antonio, TX, December 2–5, 1992).

13. T. Harford, *Adapt: Why Success Always Starts with Failure* (New York: Farrar, Straus and Giroux, 2011).

14. Ibid.

15. L. Howard, *Williams, Hegel, Heraclitus, and Marx's Dialectic* (New York: Harvester Wheatsheaf, 1989).

16. T. Harford, *Adapt: Why Success Always Starts with Failure* (New York: Farrar, Straus and Giroux, 2011).

Chapter 4

1. D. Gilbert, *Stumbling on Happiness* (New York: Knopf, 2006).

2. R. Thaler and C. Sunstein, *Nudge: Improving Decisions about Health, Wealth, and Happiness* (New York: Penguin Books, 2009).

3. G. Easterbrook, *The Progress Paradox: How Life Gets Better while People Feel Worse* (New York: Random House, 2004).

4. J. de Graaf et al., *Affluenza: The All-Consuming Epidemic* (New York: Berrett-Koehler Publishers, 2005).

5. G. Easterbrook, *The Progress Paradox: How Life Gets Better while People Feel Worse* (New York: Random House, 2004).

6. D. Gilbert, *Stumbling on Happiness* (New York: Knopf, 2006).

7. R. Williams, *Breaking Bad Habits* (Amazon Digital Services, 2011).

8. P. A. Joseph and S. Linley, "Positive Change Following Trauma and Adversity: A Review," *Journal of Trauma Stress* 17, no. 1 (February 2004), 11–21.

9. R. Tedeschi and L. Calhoun, "Post-Traumatic Growth: Conceptual Foundations and Empirical Evidence," *Psychological Inquiry* 15, no. 1 (2004), 1–18.

10. Ibid.

11. L. Vernona, J. Dillon, and A. Steiner, "Proactive Coping, Gratitude, and Post-Traumatic Stress Disorder in College Women," *Anxiety, Stress & Coping: An International Journal* 22, no. 1 (2009), 117–27.

12. P. A. Joseph and S. Linley, "Positive Change Following Trauma and Adversity: A Review," *Journal of Trauma Stress* 17, no. 1 (February 2004), 11–21.

13. A. Wood et al., "Using Personal and Psychological Strengths Leads to Increases in Well-Being over Time: A Longitudinal Study and the Development of the Strengths Use Questionnaire," *Personality and Individual Differences* 50 (2011), 15–19.

14. M. Seligman and C. Peterson, "Strengths of Character and Wellbeing," *Journal of Social and Clinical Psychology,* 23, no. 5 (2004), 603–19.

15. M. Seligman and C. Peterson, "Character Strengths before and after September 11" (research report, University of Michigan and University of Pennsylvania, 2002).

16. M. McCullough, M. Kimeldorf, and A. Cohen, "An Adaptation for Altruism? The Social Causes, Social Effects, and Social Evolution of Gratitude," *Current Directions in Psychological Science* 17, no. 4 (2008).

17. Frans de Waal, "Moral Behavior in Animals" (lecture, TEDxPeachtree, 2010).

18. F. Warneken, "The Development of Altruistic Behavior: Helping in Children and Chimpanzees," *Social Research* 80, no. 2 (2010).

19. Ibid.

20. M. McCullough, M. Kimeldorf, and A. Cohen, "An Adaptation for Altruism? The Social Causes, Social Effects, and Social Evolution of Gratitude," *Current Directions in Psychological Science* 17, no. 4 (2008).

21. A. Wood et al., "Using Personal and Psychological Strengths Leads to Increases in Well-Being over Time: A Longitudinal Study and the Development of the Strengths Use Questionnaire," *Personality and Individual Differences* 50 (2011), 15–19.

22. P. A. Joseph and S. Linley, "Positive Change Following Trauma and Adversity: A Review," *Journal of Trauma Stress* 17, no. 1 (February 2004), 11–21.

23. Ibid.

24. A. Wood, J. Froh, and A. Geraghty, "Gratitude and Well-Being: A Review and Theoretical Integration," *Clinical Psychology Review* (2010).

25. Ibid.

26. A. Wood et al., "Using Personal and Psychological Strengths Leads to Increases in Well-Being over Time: A Longitudinal Study and the Development of the Strengths Use Questionnaire," *Personality and Individual Differences* 50 (2011), 15–19.

27. P. A. Joseph and S. Linley, "Positive Change Following Trauma and Adversity: A Review," *Journal of Trauma Stress* 17, no. 1 (February 2004), 11–21.

28. Ibid.

29. Ibid.

30. Ibid.

Chapter 5

1. Diana Nyad, "Never, Ever Give Up" (lecture, TED Women, 2013).

2. Brene Brown, *Daring Greatly: How the Courage to Be Vulnerable Transforms the Way We Live, Love, Parent, and Lead* (New York: Gotham Books, 2012).

3. Tim Harford, *Adapt: Why Success Always Starts with Failure* (New York: Farrar, Straus and Giroux, 2011).

4. Richard G. Tedeschi and Lawrence G. Calhoun, "Post-traumatic Growth: Conceptual Foundations and Empirical Evidence," *Psychological Inquiry* 15, no. 1 (2004).

5. Ibid.

6. C. S. Dweck and E. L. Leggett, "A Social-Cognitive Approach to Motivation and Personality," *Psychological Review* 95 (1988), 256–73.

7. C. M. Mueller and C. S. Dweck, "Praise for Intelligence Can Undermine Children's Motivation and Performance," *Journal of Personality and Social Psychology* 75 (1998), 33–52.

8. C. S. Dweck and E. L. Leggett, "A Social-Cognitive Approach to Motivation and Personality," *Psychological Review* 95 (1988), 256–73.

9. C. M. Mueller and C. S. Dweck, "Praise for Intelligence Can Undermine Children's Motivation and Performance," *Journal of Personality and Social Psychology* 75 (1998), 33–52.

10. Ibid.

11. E. S. Elliott and C. S. Dweck, "Goals: An Approach to Motivation and Achievement," *Journal of Personality and Social Psychology* 54 (1988), 5–12.

12. C. Dweck, *Mindset: The New Psychology of Success* (New York: Random House, 2006).

13. A. Kaplan and C. Midgley, "The Effect of Achievement Goals: Does Level of Perceived Academic Competence Make a Difference?" *Contemporary Educational Psychology* 22 (1997), 415–35.

14. E. S. Elliott and C. S. Dweck, "Goals: An Approach to Motivation and Achievement," *Journal of Personality and Social Psychology* 54 (1988), 5–12.

15. C. M. Mueller and C. S. Dweck, "Praise for Intelligence Can Undermine Children's Motivation and Performance," *Journal of Personality and Social Psychology* 75 (1998), 33–52.

16. Ibid.

17. Tim Harford, *Adapt: Why Success Always Starts with Failure* (New York: Farrar, Straus and Giroux, 2011).

18. Ibid.

19. J. Fultz, M. Schaller, and R. B. Cialdini, "Empathy, Sadness and Distress: Three Related but Distinct Vicarious Affective Responses to Another's Suffering," *Personality and Social Psychology Bulletin* 14 (1988), 312–15.

20. J. Fultz et al., "Social Evaluation and the Empathy-Altruism Hypothesis," *Journal of Personality and Social Psychology* 50 (1986).

21. T. Gilovich, D. Keltner, and R. E. Nisbett, *Social Psychology* (New York: W. W. Norton, 2006).

22. C. D. Batson and L. L. Shaw, "Evidence for Altruism: Toward a Pluralism of Prosocial Motives," *Psychological Inquiry* 2 (1991), 107–22.

23. Ibid.

24. Ibid.

25. R. Sapolsky, *Why Zebras Don't Get Ulcers: The Acclaimed Guide to Stress, Stress- Related Diseases, and Coping* (New York: Holt Paperbacks, 2004).

26. Ibid.

27. J. W. Pennebaker, "Confession, Inhibition, and Disease," *Advances in Experimental Social Psychology* 22 (1989), 211–44.

28. D. Mechanic and J. Tanner, "Vulnerable People, Groups, and Populations: Societal View," *Health Affairs* 26, no. 5 (September 2007), 1220–30.

29. Richard G. Tedeschi and Lawrence G. Calhoun, "Post-traumatic Growth: Conceptual Foundations and Empirical Evidence," *Psychological Inquiry* 15, no. 1 (2004).

30. Ibid.

Chapter 6

1. D. M. Wegner and S. Zanakos, "Chronic Thought Suppression," *Journal of Personality* 62 (1994), 615–40.

2. P. Seltzer, "Why We Hide Emotional Pain," *Psychology Today,* September 28, 2011.

3. Ibid.

4. P. Gilbert, *Shame: Interpersonal Behavior, Psychopathology and Culture* (New York: Oxford University Press, 1998).

5. M. Matos, J. Pinto-Gouviea, and V. Costa, "Understanding the Importance of Attachment in Shame Traumatic Memory Relation to Depression: The Impact of Emotion Regulation Processes," *Clinical Psychology and Psychotherapy* (2011): doi: 10.1002/cpp.786.

6. J. Freyd, "Definition of Betrayal Trauma," Dynamic.uoregon.edu.

7. P. Gilbert, *Shame: Interpersonal Behavior, Psychopathology and Culture* (New York: Oxford University Press, 1998).

8. Richard G. Tedeschi and Lawrence G. Calhoun, "Post-traumatic Growth: A New Perspective on Psychotraumatology," *Psychiatric Times* 64, no. 2 (2004): 165–71.

9. R. G. Tedeschi and L. G. Calhoun, "Post-traumatic Growth: Conceptual Foundations and Empirical Evidence," *Psychological Inquiry* 15, no. 1 (2004).

10. J. W. Pennebaker, "Confronting a Traumatic Event: Toward an Understanding of Inhibition and Disease," *Journal of Abnormal Psychology* 95, no. 3 (1986), 274–81.

11. Ibid.

12. K. Glassman, "Trauma and Relationships," (2005), www.istss.org.

13. Richard G. Tedeschi and Lawrence G. Calhoun, "Post-traumatic Growth: A New Perspective on Psychotraumatology," *Psychiatric Times* 64, no. 2 (2004): 165–71.

14. R. I. M. Dunbar, "The Social Role of Touch in Humans and Primates: Behavioural Function and Neurobiological Mechanisms," *Neuroscience and Biobehavioral Reviews* 34 (2010), 260–68.

15. J. B. Silk, S. C. Alberts, and J. Altmann, "Social Bonds of Female Baboons Enhance Infant Survival," *Science* 302 (2003), 1231–34.

16. R. I. M. Dunbar, "The Social Role of Touch in Humans and Primates: Behavioural Function and Neurobiological Mechanisms," *Neuroscience and Biobehavioral Reviews* 34 (2010), 260–68.

17. Ibid.

18. E. B. Keverne, N. Martensz, and B. Tuite, "Beta-endorphin Concentrations in Cerebrospinal Fluid of Monkeys Are Influenced by Grooming Relationships," *Psychoneuroendocrinology* 14 (1989), 155–61.

19. R. I. M. Dunbar, "The Social Role of Touch in Humans and Primates: Behavioural Function and Neurobiological Mechanisms," *Neuroscience and Biobehavioral Reviews* 34 (2010), 260–68.

20. G. Stefano et al., "Endogenous Morphine," *Trends in Neuroscience* 23 (2000), 436–42.

21. Ibid.

22. J. D. Belluzzi and L. Stein, "Enkephalin May Mediate Euphoria and Drive-Reduction Reward," *Nature* 266 (1977), 556–58.

23. E. E. Nelson and J. Panksepp, "Brain Structures of Infant–Mother Attachment: Contributions of Opioids, Oxytocin, and Norepinephrine," *Neuroscience and Biobehavioral Reviews* 22 (1998), 437–52.

24. T. R. Insel and L. E. Shapiro, "Oxytocin Receptor Distribution Reflects Social Organisation in Monogamous and Polygamous Voles," *PNAS* 89 (1992), 5981–85.

25. T. R. Insel and L. J. Young, "Neuropeptides and the Evolution of Social Behavior," *Current Opinions in Neurobiology* 10 (2000), 784–89.

26. J. R. Williams et al., "Oxytocin Centrally Administered Facilitates formation of a Partner Preference in Prairie Voles (Microtus ochrogaster)," *Journal of Neuroendocrinology* 6 (1994), 153–63.

27. J. T. Winslow et al., "A Role for Central Vasopressin in Pair Bonding in Monogamous Voles," *Nature* 365 (1993), 545–48.

28. L. J. Young, "Oxytocin and Vasopressin Receptors and Species-Typical Social Behaviors," *Hormones and Behavior* 36 (1999), 212–21.

29. T. R. Insel and T. J. Hulihan, "A Gender Specific Mechanism for Pair Bonding: Oxytocin and Partner Preference Formation in Monogamous Voles," *Behavioral Neuroscience* 109 (1995), 782–89.

30. M. M. Cho et al., "The Effects of Oxytocin and Vasopressin on Partner Preference in Male and Female Coles (Microtus ochrogaster)," *Behavioral Neuroscience* 113 (1999), 1071–79.

31. C. S. Carter, A. C. DeVries, and L. L. Getz, "Physiological Substrates of Mammalian Monogamy: The Prairie Vole Model," *Neuroscience and Biobehavioral Review* 16 (1995), 131–44.

32. J. A. Amico et al., "Anxiety and Stress Responses in Female Oxytocin Deficient Mice," *Journal of Neuroendocrinology* 16 (2004), 319–24.

33. K. Uvnäs-Moberg, "Oxytocin May Mediate the Benefits of Positive Social Interaction and Emotions," *Psychoneuroendocrinology* 23 (1998), 819–35.

34. M. Peterssen et al., "Oxytocin Causes a Long-Term Decrease of Blood Pressure in Female and Male Rats," *Physiology and Behavior* 60 (1998a), 1311–15.

35. M. Peterssen et al., "Oxytocin Increases Nociceptive Pain Threshold in a Long-Term Perspective in Female and Male Rats," *Neuroscience* 212 (1998b), 87–90.

Chapter 7

1. A. Newberg and M. Waldman, *How God Changes Your Brain: Breakthrough Finding from a Leading Neuroscientist* (New York: Ballantine Books, 2010).

2. S. Pappas, "Feeling Down? Spirituality Can Boost Your Mood," *LiveScience*, September 28, 2012.

3. J. D. Creswell et al., "Neural Correlates of Dispositional Mindfulness during Affect Labeling," *Psychosomatic Medicine* 69, no. 6 (Jul–Aug 2007), 560–65.

4. T. W. Kjaer et al., "Increased Dopamine Tone during Meditation-Induced Change of Consciousness," *Brain Research Cognitive Brain Research* 13, no. 2 (April 2002), 255–59.

5. C. C. Streeter et al., "Yoga Asana Sessions Increase Brain GABA Levels: A Pilot Study," *Journal of Alternative and Complementary Medicine* 13, no. 4 (May 2007), 419–26.

6. J. R. Infante et al., "Catecholamine Levels in Practitioners of the Transcendental Meditation Technique," *Physiology & Behavior* 72, no. 1-2 (January 2001), 141–46.

7. M. Seligman, *Learned Optimism: How to Change Your Mind and Your Life* (New York: Vintage Books, 2006).

8. J. A. Brefczynski-Lewis et al., "Neural Correlates of Attentional Expertise in Long-Term Meditation Practitioners," *PNAS* 104, no. 27 (July 3, 2007), 11483–88.

9. Davidson, R.; Lutz, A. (2008). "Buddha's Brain: Neuroplasticity and Meditation In The Spotlight." IEEE *Signal Processing Magazine* 25 (1): 174-176

10. A. R. Isaac, "Mental Practice—Does It Work in the Field?," *The Sport Psychologist* 6 (1992), 192–98.

11. R. Roure et al., "Autonomic Nervous System Responses Correlate with Mental Rehearsal in Volleyball Training," *Journal of Applied Physiology* 78, no. 2 (1998), 99–108.

12. K. A. Martin and C. R. Hall, "Using Mental Imagery to Enhance Intrinsic Motivation," *Journal of Sport and Exercise Psychology* 17, no. 1 (1995), 54–69.

13. T. Toneatto and L. Nguyen, "Does Mindfulness Mediation Improve Anxiety and Mood Symptoms? A Review of Controlled Research," *Canadian Journal of Psychiatry* 52, no. 4 (April 2007), 240–46.

14. S. Pappas, "Feeling Down? Spirituality Can Boost Your Mood," *LiveScience*, September 28, 2012.

15. A. Newberg and M. Waldman, *How God Changes Your Brain: Breakthrough Finding from a Leading Neuroscientist* (New York: Ballantine Books, 2010).

16. Ibid.

17. Ibid.

18. Ibid.

19. Lamm, C., Batson, C.D., Decety, J., (2007). The neural substrate of human empathy: effects of perspective taking and cognitive appraisal. *Journal of Cognitive Neuroscience*. 2007 Jan; 19 (1):42-28

20. A. Newberg and M. Waldman, *How God Changes Your Brain: Breakthrough Finding from a Leading Neuroscientist* (New York: Ballantine Books, 2010).

21. Ibid.

22. Taylor, B. (2008). *The Encyclopedia of Religion and Nature*. New York, Bloomsbury Academic.

23. Ibid.

24. Akeley, C., Akeley, D. (2008). J. T. Jr: *The Biology Of An African Monkey*. New York, Litereary Licensing LLC.

25. Balcombe, J. (2011). *Second Nature: The Inner Lives of Animals*. New York, Palgrave, Macmillan Trade.

26. Ibid.

27. Rudeman, P.H., Walton, M.E., Millette, B.H., Shirley, E., Rushworth, M.F., Bannerman, D.M. (2007). Distinct contributions of frontal areas to emotion and social behavior in the rat. *European Journal of Neuroscience.* 2007 Oct; 26(8);2315-26

28. Milad, M.R., Quirk, G.J., Pitman, R.K., Orr, S.P., Fischl, B., Rauch, S.L., (2007). A role for the human dorsal anterior cingulated cortex in fear expression. *Biological Psychiatry.* 2007 Aug 16.

29. Pappas, S. (2012). Feeling Down? Spirituality Can Boost your Mood. *LiveScience.* 2012, Sep 28

30. Drescher, K., Foy, D. When They Come Home: Posttraumatic Stress, Moral Injury, and Spiritual Consequences for Veterans. Retreived, February, 3, 2015 at www.http://journals.sfu.ca/rpfs/index.php/rpfs/article/viewFile/158/157

31. Ibid

32. Tedeschi, R.G., and Calhoun, L.G. (2004). Post-traumatic growth: Conceptual foundations and empirical evidence. Psychological Inquiry, 15, 1

33. Ibid

34. Ibid

Section Two

1. Hofstede, Geert. (1993). *Cultures and Organizations: Software of the Mind. Administrative Science Quarterly* (Johnson Graduate School of Management, Cornell University) 38 (1): 132-134. JSTOR 2393257

2. Achor, S. (2010). *The Happinness Advantage: The Seven Priniciplesof Positive Psychology That Fuel Success and Performance at Work.* New York, Crown Business

41768775R00093

Made in the USA
Lexington, KY
27 May 2015